Modern English Syntax

Modern English Syntax

C. T. Onions

New edition of *An Advanced English Syntax,* prepared from the author's materials by

B. D. H. Miller

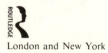

London and New York

This edition first published in Great Britain 1971
Reprinted and first published as a paperback 1974
Reprinted 1978, 1980 and 1985
by Routledge & Kegan Paul

Reprinted 1989 and 1993 by Routledge
11 New Fetter Lane, London EC4P 4EE

This edition © Routledge 1971

First edition, under the title *An Advanced English Syntax*, 1904
Second edition 1905
Third edition 1911
Fourth edition 1927
Fifth edition 1929
Sixth edition 1932
This edition (completely revised) 1971

Printed in Great Britain by T. J. Press (Padstow) Ltd., Cornwall

ISBN 0–415–05074–X

Contents

Preface

Charles Talbut Onions, last surviving editor of the *Oxford English Dictionary*, editor of *A Shakespeare Glossary* (1911), the *Shorter Oxford English Dictionary* (1933), and the *Oxford Dictionary of English Etymology* (1966), and long *facile princeps* of English lexicographers, died in January 1965, aged 91. For many years, almost up to the time of his death, he had been making notes for a revised edition of *An Advanced English Syntax*; among his literary remains were six copies of the book more or less heavily annotated, a number of sections apparently in final draft, and more than 500 scraps of paper, of every shape and size, each containing anything from one to several dozen memoranda of words, phrases, or constructions.

From this bulk of largely undigested material I have tried to make, within the limits prescribed, something approximating to the book that Dr Onions might himself have produced; to allow room for new material I have omitted the final sections, on parataxis and hypotaxis. In this undertaking I have been helped by Dr Onions's executors, who kindly gave me unrestricted use of the manuscript material, and by the publishers, who readily acceded to my suggestions; to both I offer my thanks.

Brasenose College   B. D. H. Miller
Oxford

Original preface to *An Advanced English Syntax*

The object of this short treatise is to present the main facts of current English syntax in a systematic form in accordance with the principles of the Parallel Grammar Series. The introduction is designed to provide a full scheme of sentence analysis. The rest of the book—the syntax proper—is arranged in two parts. Part I contains a treatment of syntactical phenomena based on the analysis of sentences. Part II classifies the uses of forms. Cross references indicate how the two parts of syntax supplement one another. . . .

While dealing mainly with the language of the present day, I have endeavoured to make the book of use to the student of early modern English by giving an account of some notable archaic and obsolete constructions. Historical matter has been introduced wherever it was considered necessary for the understanding of important points in syntax-development or seemed to add interest to the treatment of particular constructions.

Of the existing grammars which I have consulted, Dr Sweet's has proved the most enlightening and suggestive.

My connexion with the *Oxford English Dictionary* has given me facilities for research which I should otherwise not have had, and I wish to thank the editors of that work for the assistance which they have, directly or indirectly, afforded me in my task.

To Dr Henry Bradley I am especially indebted for valuable suggestions and emendations, in both the manuscript and the proof stages of the book.

To Dr Sonnenschein, my former professor, I am grateful for his constant help and stimulating criticism throughout my work.

Oxford,   C. T. Onions
10th September, 1903

It is customary to recognize

Three main periods of English

Old English (abbreviated OE.), from about AD 700 to about AD 1100. Period of full vowels in the endings, e.g. far*a*n, sun*u*, wulf*a*s.

Middle English (abbreviated ME.), from about AD 1100 to about AD 1500. The full vowels in the endings are weakened to one uniform unstressed *e*, e.g. far*e*n, son*e*, wolv*e*s.

Modern English (abbreviated ModE.), from about AD 1500 to the present day. The unstressed *e* in the endings has become silent, and has often disappeared from the written word, e.g. far*e*, son, wolv*e*s.

Introduction

Analysis of sentences

---

1   Speech is made up of sentences.

A **sentence** [Latin *sententia* 'meaning'] is a group of words, or sometimes a single word, which makes—

    (i) a **statement**; e.g. I am an Englishman.

or (ii) a **command** or an **expression of wish**; e.g.

      Open the window.   Let us go.

or (iii) a **question**; e.g. How do you do?

or (iv) an **exclamation**; e.g. How it thunders! What a blow!

Compare §§48–57.

Many single words or self-contained groups of words, of any size, may perform the work of a sentence; e.g. Speaking; Thanks; Down!; Sh!; Out with it!; Farewell; Goodbye; What?; Murder!; Nonsense!; Splendid!

'Yes' and 'no' are long-established sentence-words; they are words *equivalent* to sentences; e.g. 'Will you come?'—'Yes' (= I will come). Other words which may be equivalent to sentences will be mentioned below (§4).

2   **Analysis** means *breaking up* [Greek *ana* 'up' and *lysis* 'breaking'], and is the name given to the process of breaking up a sentence into its parts. On pp. 1 to 22 it will be shown how to *analyse* sentences.

There are sentences in English and other languages which it is very difficult, or impossible, to analyse grammatically. But analysis may be applied to the majority of sentences and without it we should be unable to recognize the peculiarities of those sentences which cannot be analysed.

3   The first stage in the analysis of a sentence is into:

    1 the **subject**   2 the **predicate.**

The **subject** denotes **the person or thing about which something is said** by means of the predicate.

The **predicate** is **what is said** about the person or thing denoted by the subject.

In the following examples of sentences the part printed in roman type is the subject; the part printed in italics is the predicate.

> The few *are happy*. *Long live* the Queen!
> Who *knows*? Who *goes there*?
> *Be* it *so*.
> *How beautiful* she *looks*!
> Fools *rush in where angels fear to tread*.—POPE
> *Uneasy lies* the head that wears a crown.—SHAKESPEARE
> He *laughs best* who laughs last.
> A terrible accident *has happened*.
> Whatever is, *is right*.—POPE
> *Listen.* ⎱ (The subject 'thou', 'ye', or 'you' is not
> *Do not go.* ⎰ expressed.)

4 Some sentences lack some part or parts that are ideally necessary to the full form of a sentence as defined above. These are called *elliptical* sentences, and an **ellipsis** is said to occur. Ellipsis plays a great part in English as in many languages. It is common to all styles of speaking and writing. In poetical and rhetorical language it often lends dignity and impressiveness, with something of an archaic flavour; to colloquial speech it gives precision and brevity, and saves time and trouble. It is especially appropriate to exclamations and abrupt commands. Examples:

> To err is human, to forgive divine.—POPE (Supply 'is')
> One murder makes a villain, a million a hero. (Supply 'make')
> This house to be let or sold. (Supply 'is')
> Students must be able to help, and we hope will. (Supply 'help')
> Go and see what the boy's doing, and tell him not to. (Supply 'do it')
> Rest assured that everything will be done that can be. (Supply 'done')
> You are more likely to quarrel with me than I with you. (i.e. than I am likely to quarrel with you)
> Well roared, Lion: well run, Thisbe.—SHAKESPEARE

Thy name well fits thy faith; thy faith thy name.—
  SHAKESPEARE (Supply 'well fits')
Thank you. (=I thank you: cf. German *danke*)
Your name and address, please. (i.e. Give me your name)
What if he dies? (=What will happen, *or* What will you do
  or say if he dies?)
I could, but I won't. (e.g. do it)
Is the venture a success, and if not, why not?
(At the railway booking office) Oxford, second, single.
One master or many.
Easier said than done.
Once an actor, always an actor.
Here goes! Never again.
Fire, fire! Silence!
Hats off! What a pity!
Well, I never!

Ellipsis is very common in answers where the complete form of
the answer reflects that of the question and is therefore sufficiently
obvious not to require full expression. Examples:

Who did it?—I. (i.e. did it)
How many were saved?—Twenty. (i.e. were saved)
Have you ever been abroad?—Never. (i.e. have I been
  abroad)
We will send somebody.—Whom? When? Where to?
  (i.e. will you send?)

Similarly with all interrogative words.

Ellipsis is common also in wishes, as 'good morning'; 'bless
you'; 'all good wishes'.

Ellipsis enters into the development of various conversational
or unstudied formulas; e.g. all right; not at all; no doubt; half a
minute; one moment, please; all the same . . .; let alone . . .;
no matter who (what, when) . . .; no wonder; . . . and no
mistake; far from it; and a good thing too.

Numerals are used in many kinds of elliptical constructions:
e.g. a child of *five* [years of age]; between *a quarter* [of an hour]
and *ten* [minutes] to *five* [o'clock]; from *four* [o'clock] to
half [an hour] *past* [four]; the *first* [day] of April; a *tenth*
[part] of a pound; a coach and *four* [horses].

Single words like 'Good!' 'Right!' 'Now!' 'Really?' 'Certainly'; 'Granted'; 'True'; 'Quick!' 'Enough!' are often equivalent to sentences.

Instances like the following, where a verb of motion in the infinitive is omitted, belong to older stages of the language:

> I must to Coventry.—SHAKESPEARE, *Richard II*
> He to England shall along with you.—*Hamlet*
> I shall no more to sea.—*Tempest*
> I wylle to morowe to the cowrte of Kyng Arthur.—MALORY

This usage is regular in OE. with the so-called 'auxiliaries': *Ic tō sǣ wille* = 'I to sea will [go]'.

5 The five forms of the predicate

Most predicates contain a verb, which is the medium by which the predication is normally conveyed.

The predicate may consist of—

    1   a verb only
    2   a verb together with some other word or words.

Sentences are classified according to the form of the predicate, which may assume any of *five* principal forms.

First form of the predicate

Subject	Predicate
Day	dawns
He	died
My hour	is come
The shades of night	were falling

In such sentences the predicate consists of the **verb alone.**

6 *Second form of the predicate*

Subject	Predicate	
	verb	*predicative adjective* or *predicative noun* or *predicative pronoun*
Croesus	was	rich *or* a king
Many	lay	dead
I	am	he
Thought	is	free
Seeing	is	believing
To err	is	human
The meeting	stands	adjourned
We	are getting	ready

In such sentences the predicate consists of (1) a **verb,** and (2) a **predicative adjective, predicative noun,** or **predicative pronoun,** i.e. an adjective, noun, or pronoun *predicated of the subject*. This form of the predicate embraces the participles used in constructing compound tenses, e.g. 'was coming', 'were ruined'. Observe that here and in the fifth form of the predicate the verb and the predicative word or words form a unity ('lie dead', 'stand adjourned', 'get ready') in which the verb often acquires an extended meaning not shown when the verb is not thus linked. Cf. *run short, come clean, come undone*.

For the kinds of verbs that may be used in a predicate of the second form, see §35.

7   In a sentence like 'It is hard to do right', the pronoun *it* is called the **formal subject** (or 'anticipatory subject') because, although it is a subject in *form*, it merely anticipates or provisionally represents the real subject, which follows. Thus we have a predicate of the second form:

| To do right (It) | is | hard. |

For the relation between this *it* and the *it* which forms the subject of impersonal verbs, see §171.4.

In sentences like 'There was peace', 'there was' is equivalent to 'existed', 'came into existence', and we have in origin a predicate of the first form containing an adjunct (§15):

Peace | was (*verb*) there (*adjunct*, §15).

There, however, has become formal.

8   *Third form of the predicate*

Subject	Predicate	
	verb	*object*
Rats	desert	a sinking ship
Many hands	make	light work
Nobody	wishes	to know
He	can (§40)	tell
You	would have	what me do
They	do think	what we are

In such sentences the predicate consists of (1) a **verb,** and (2) an **object,** which denotes the person or thing to which the action of the verb 'passes over'.

Verbs taking an object are called **transitive** [= 'passing over', Latin *transire* 'to pass over']. Verbs not taking an object are called **intransitive** [= 'not passing over'].

For the *cognate object* see §37.

Note that tabular analysis does not distinguish different kinds of sentence, e.g. statement and question. The fourth sentence above might be read either: 'He can tell' (statement) or: 'Can he tell?' (question); the last two sentences are both questions: 'What would you have me do?'; 'What do they think we are?'

9   When a sentence with a predicate of the third form is turned into the passive, we have a sentence with a predicate of the first form containing an adjunct (§15); e.g. 'Cain killed Abel' becomes:

Subject	Predicate
Abel	was killed (*verb*) by Cain (*adjunct*)

10   *Fourth form of the predicate*

Subject	Predicate		
	verb	*two objects*	
We	taught	the dog	tricks
I	ask	you	this question
They	showed	me	the way
We	asked	him	to speak

In such sentences the predicate consists of (1) a **verb,** and (2) **two objects.**

For the kinds of verbs which may be used in a predicate of the fourth form, see §41.1.

A sentence like 'I gave **him** the money' may be regarded in two ways:

(a) In form, it is like 'We ask you this' or 'I asked him a question'; hence *him*, which is in form a dative, is often called an object (**indirect object**).

(b) In meaning, the sentence is equivalent to 'I gave the money **to him**', which is most simply parsed as containing an adjunct (§15) in a predicate of the third form.

Sentences like 'We asked *him to speak*' may also be analysed as containing a predicate of the third form (subject *we*, verb *asked*, object *him to speak = that he should speak*).

11 When a sentence with a predicate of the fourth form is turned into the passive, we get a sentence with a predicate of the third form containing an adjunct (§15); e.g. 'You ask me my opinion', 'I told him to speak', become:

Subject	Predicate		
	verb	*object retained*	*adjunct*
I	am asked	my opinion	by you
He	was told	to speak	by me

12 *Fifth form of the predicate*

Subject	Predicate		
	verb	*object*	*predicative adjective or predicative noun*
Nothing	makes	a Stoic	angry
People	called	Duns Scotus	the Subtle Doctor
They	elected	him	Consul
He	thought	himself	a happy man
The thought	drove	him	mad
	Leave	me	alone

In such sentences the predicate consists of (1) a **verb**, (2) an **object**, and (3) a **predicative adjective** or **predicative noun**, i.e. an adjective or noun *predicated of the object*.

Note that in commands and prohibitions (e.g. 'Leave me **alone**') no subject is expressed.

For the kinds of verbs used in a predicate of the fifth form, see §§44–5.

13 When a sentence with a predicate of the fifth form is turned into the passive, we get a sentence with a predicate of the second form containing an adjunct (§15); e.g. 'The Court declared him a traitor' becomes:

Subject	Predicate		
	verb	*predicative adjective or noun*	*adjunct*
He	was declared	a traitor	by the Court

14 Attributes
A noun may be **qualified** by an adjective (or adjective-equivalent, §18); e.g. *dear* friends; *a good* man; *my* father; *ten* men.
    Such a qualifying part of a sentence is called an **attribute.**

15 Adjuncts
A verb, an adjective, or an adverb may be **qualified** by an adverb (or adverb-equivalent, §19); e.g. Fight *bravely*; He is *quite* happy; *Well* begun is *half* done.
    Such a qualifying part of a sentence is called an **adjunct.** For instances in the various forms of the predicate, see §24.1.

16 Equivalents
The noun, the adjective, and the adverb may be replaced by other parts of speech doing the same work in the sentence, or by a group of words doing the work of a single part of speech.
    A word or group of words which functions as a noun, an adjective, or an adverb is called an **equivalent** (noun-equivalent, adjective-equivalent, or adverb-equivalent).
    A group of words forming an equivalent and not having a subject and predicate of its own is called a **phrase**. Cf. §§18.5, 19.1.
    A group of words forming an equivalent and having a subject and predicate of its own is called a **subordinate clause**. Cf. §21.

17 *Noun-equivalents*
A noun-equivalent may be provided by:

(1) a pronoun:
>The boy is here; *he* has not been long.
>*You* are fortunate, *I* am wretched.
>*It* is *I*.

(2) a verb-noun:
>*To see* is *to believe*. *Seeing* is *believing*.
>I desire *to learn*. His frequent *comings* and *goings*.

Note—A verb-noun participates in all the constructions of the verb to which it belongs. Thus it may take a predicative adjective, predicative noun, or predicative pronoun; or an object; or two objects; or an object and a predicative adjective or noun; and it may be qualified by an adverb—just like a verb.

(3) an adjective or adjectival phrase (with or without *the*; see §184):
>at *dead* of night
>through *thick* and *thin*
>the *careful*, the *careless*, the *indifferent*, the *brave*, the *callous*
>*all* and *sundry*
>*Fair's* fair.
>the survival of the *fittest*
>Things went from *bad* to *worse*.
>the *next-of-kin*

(4) a verb-adjective (sometimes with *the*):
>(the) *living* and (the) *dead*   *killed* and *wounded*
>the *fallen*   both teachers and *taught*

(5) an adverb or adverbial phrase:
>Up to *now*; from *now* on; till *then*; every *so often*; for *once*; for *ever*; from *here* to *there*; from *abroad*; from *beyond the sea*; I like *abroad*; out of the *everywhere* into *here*.

(6) a clause (in a complex sentence, §20):
>*That you have wronged me* doth appear in this.—SHAKESPEARE
>Who knows *how it happened*? Tell me *what you mean*.

(7) a word or group of words quoted, or used as subject, object, or predicate:
>'*And*' is a conjunction. '*I think not*' was all he said.
>But me no *buts*.   There is much virtue in '*if*'.
>the *when* and *how* of pruning
>a matter of *give-and-take*

(8) a sentence:

Why haven't you been to see me since *I don't know when*?
(Cf. the sentences 'Forget me not', 'Love lies bleeding', which
have become, as names of flowers, a single word.)

In sentences like *'Through the wood* is the nearest way', *'From Tamworth thither* is but one day's march' (Shakespeare), a phrase formed with
a preposition would seem to stand as a noun-equivalent. But this is not
really so; the sentences are inverted forms of 'The nearest way is through
the wood', 'It is but one day's march from Tamworth thither'.

18 *Adjective-equivalents*

An adjective-equivalent may be provided by:

(1) a verb-adjective:

a *running* sore   a *printed* book
The city lies *sleeping*.

Note—A verb-adjective participates in all the constructions of
the verb to which it belongs. Thus it may take a predicative
adjective, predicative noun, or predicative pronoun; or an object;
or two objects; or an object and a predicative adjective or
predicative noun; and it may be qualified by an adverb—just
like a verb.

(2) a noun in apposition, i.e. a noun, with or without epithet,
describing or identifying:

We *English*   Prince *Consort*
King Alfred   Simon Lee, the old *huntsman*
London town (cf. 5)

(3) a noun in the genitive case:

Milton's works   *Duncan's* murderer
today's news (= German 'die *heutigen* Nachrichten')
a *summer's* day
the *Queen's* palace (= the *royal* palace)
Cicero's treatise on friendship (cf. the *Ciceronian* treatise)
Plato's doctrine of ideas (= the *Platonic* doctrine)

(4) a noun in the accusative case, qualified, forming a descriptive
expression ('accusative of description'):

a book *the same size as this*
water *the colour of pea-soup*

These equivalents are most often used like predicative adjectives:

The earth is *the shape of an orange* (= orange-shaped).
What age is he? (= how old?)

For more examples, see §106.

(5) a phrase formed with a preposition:
a lump *of lead* (= a *leaden* lump)
men *of honour* (= *honourable* men)
a place *of safety* (= a *safe* place)
ten years *of age* (= ten years *old*)
the City *of London* (cf. 2)
towns *by the sea* (= *maritime* towns)
a wind *from the north* (= a *northerly* wind)
the way *through the wood*
the day *after tomorrow*
the philosophy *of Kant* (= *Kantian* philosophy)
the man *in the street*
men *at work*
times *without number*
books *about Oxford*
A bird *in the hand* is worth two *in the bush.*
years *to come* (= *future* years)

(6) a noun or verb-noun forming part of a compound noun:
cannon balls (= balls *for cannon*; see 5 above)
walking sticks (= sticks *for walking*)
head wind (= a wind *from the front*)
sick room (= the room *for the sick*; see 5 above and §17.3.
    Cf. sick bay, -bed, -benefit, -call, -list.)

DEFINITION—**A compound noun** consists of two nouns (or of a noun and a verb-noun) the first of which is an attribute of the second. The two nouns may be written either as two distinct words, or as two words joined by a hyphen, or as a single word; e.g. *lunatic asylum—dancing lesson—sheep-dog—milkmaid.* That the first part of such compounds is a noun (and not an adjective) is shown by the meaning. A *lunatic asylum* does not mean an *asylum that is insane,* but an *asylum for the insane.* So a *walking stick* means a *stick used in walking,* not a *stick that walks,* a *dancing master* means a *master for dancing,* a *dancing lesson* means a *lesson in dancing.*

Sometimes it is uncertain whether the qualifying word ending in *–ing* is a verb-noun or a verb-adjective; e.g. a *driving belt* may mean either a belt *that drives* (the machinery) or a belt *for driving* it. So with *hunting dog, serving man, dispensing power.*

Relations between the components of a compound noun are very various in character; cf. drinking water, drinking bout, wine and spirit merchant, loving cup, parting words, climbing accident, trouser leg, return journey, dying breath, dying day, dead march,

laughing matter, fellow man, living standards, living wage, boiling (starting, bursting) point, shopping hours, standing room,
voting powers, evening dress, washing day.

A compound noun may itself be used as an attribute and thus
form another compound noun, e.g. *drawing-room furniture*. In
this way long compound nouns are formed, such as *Commons
Enclosure Consolidation Act*. Such nouns are extremely common
in newspaper headlines; e.g. *Sunday Trading Test Case Decision*;
Ban on Sunday Cooking Plan (= plan for a ban on Sunday
cooking).

(7) an adverb or adverbial phrase:
  an *inside* passenger   the *off* side
  the *then* King   *about* to fall
  the houses (*over*) *there*   the windows *just under the cupola*
  the *above* quotations

(8) a clause (in a complex sentence, §20):
  This is the house *that Jack built*.

'The house that Jack built' is as though one said 'the house
built by Jack' or 'the Jack-built house'.

(9) a group of words preceding and qualifying the noun:
  the *seven times* table
  our *past-cure* malady—SHAKESPEARE
  a *who's afraid* sort of bearing—DICKENS
  this low *pounds-shillings-and-pence* point of view—SOUTHEY

19 *Adverb-equivalents*
An adverb-equivalent may be provided by:

(1) a phrase formed with a preposition:
  He hunts *in the woods*.
  That is good *for nothing*.
  by no means beautiful (= an emphatic *not*)
  He came *to see*. (= *for seeing*, i.e. *in order to see*)

(2) a noun, qualified or unqualified, without a preposition
(accusative of time, distance, &c., §105):
  I am going *home*. (= *towards home*   direction)
  I have walked *miles*. (distance)
  I shall not be *a moment*. (time how long)
  He died *last night*. (time when)
  a *great deal* bigger (quantity)

(3) a verb-noun:
  boiling (*scorching, steaming*) hot   *raving* mad

(4) a phrase not introduced by a preposition:
    He went *cap in hand.*
    They walked *arm in arm.*
(5) a noun or pronoun in the dative case, denoting the person interested or for whom something is done (§§120–6):
    Give *him* (or *the man*) some money.
(6) a demonstrative pronoun, or *the* with a comparative:
    this big   *that* small
    the longer *the* better
(7) an adjective describing temporal or relative status, and for the most part of ultimately Latin origin, followed by a preposition:
    To act *consistent with* himself an hour—POPE

Cf. contrary, preparatory, pursuant, relative, subject, subsequent to; independent, irrespective, regardless of; consequent upon.
(8) a clause (in a complex sentence, §20):
    I will tell you *when you come back.*

20   Simple, compound, and complex sentences

A **simple** sentence contains only one predication (= group of words having a subject and a predicate):
    This is my house.

A **compound** sentence contains two or more predications connected by *and, or,* or *nor*:
    This is my house and that (is) yours.

A **complex** sentence contains one or more predications, called dependent or subordinate *clauses,* dependent on a main (principal) predication, or main clause:

main clause	*subordinate clause*
This is the house	that Jack built

21 A **clause** is a group of words forming part of a sentence and having a subject and a predicate of its own.

A subordinate clause is of the nature of a single part of speech, noun, adjective, or adverb. It may stand in a sentence as

(1) subject; e.g. *That you have wronged me* doth appear in this.
(2) predicative noun; e.g. My comfort is *that heaven will take our souls.*
(3) object; e.g. In sooth I know not *why I am so sad.*
(4) attribute; e.g. The man *that hath no music in himself . . .*
    Is fit for treasons, stratagems, and spoils.
(5) adverbial adjunct; e.g. I am never merry *when I hear sweet music.*

(The above quotations are all from Shakespeare.)

22 Kinds of subordinate clause

Subordinate clauses may be classified according to the *part of speech* of which they are equivalents, as:

1 **noun clauses,** i.e. clauses playing the part of a noun (§17.6). These will be treated in §§58–72.

2 **adjective clauses,** i.e. clauses playing the part of an adjective (§18.8). These will be treated in §§73–9.

3 **adverb clauses,** i.e. clauses playing the part of an adverb (§19.8). These will be treated in §§80–100.

23 Co-ordination and subordination

1 Two or more sentences, clauses, phrases, or single words, linked together by one of the conjunctions

   and, but, or, nor, for, yet, only

are called **co-ordinate,** i.e. of the same rank; and the conjunctions which link them together are called **co-ordinating conjunctions:**

  (i) linking together sentences:

  God made the country, **and** *man made the town.*—COWPER

  Small showers last long, **but** *sudden storms are short.*—SHAKESPEARE

  He has said nothing, **nor** *will he.*

  Cast thy bread upon the waters, **for** *thou shalt find it after many days.*—Bible

  I would come, **only** *I am busy.*

  (ii) linking together clauses:

  The judge said *the case was a difficult one* **and** *he would reserve judgment.*

  Thou shalt speak my words to them, *whether they will hear* **or** *whether they will forbear.*—Bible

  (iii) linking together phrases, or single words:

  Darby **and** *Joan* are a happy pair.

  A youth *to fortune* **and** *to fame* unknown.—GRAY

  He delivered a *powerful* **but** *ill-tempered* speech.

  To be **or** *not to be*—that is the question.—SHAKESPEARE

In an enumeration or a succession of words or phrases it is usual to place a co-ordinating conjunction before the last of these:

  An old, mad, blind, despised, **and** dying king—SHELLEY

In modern English prose *for* (unlike the other co-ordinating conjunctions) can link together sentences only.

In a sentence like—*This is what I think,* but *I shall be glad to be corrected if I am wrong,* we have two *complex* sentences co-ordinated by *but.*

2 The first members of a group linked together by one of the above conjunctions may be preceded by a word which as it were duplicates the force of the conjunction and so brings out more clearly the relation of the two groups. Thus we have the following pairs:

both . . . and . . .
either . . . or . . .
neither . . . nor . . .
not only . . . but (also) . . .

Both, either, neither are clearly not conjunctions, for the work of a co-ordinating conjunction is to link a group which precedes to a group which follows it. These words, which serve to bind closer two words or groups linked by a co-ordinating conjunction, may be called co-ordinating adverbs.

3 All other conjunctions are **subordinating conjunctions,** introducing either noun clauses (§58) or adverb clauses (§80).

But *whether . . . or . . .*, when used without a finite verb, may have a co-ordinating effect:

Whether true *or* false, the report will be believed.

This is really a case of ellipsis, 'whether true or false' standing for 'whether it be true or false' (conditional clause, §91.5). Note that the omission of *whether*, though awkward, would not affect the meaning.

4 Words like *therefore, however, nevertheless, so, else, accordingly, hence, also, too, likewise, moreover, still,* though some of them frequently come at the beginning of a sentence, are not really conjunctions, but adverbs: their function is not that of linking. They qualify the sentence as a whole rather than any particular part of it, and may therefore be called sentence adverbs.

Ordinary adverbs in *-ly* which may be used thus are *actually, admittedly, allegedly, apparently, assuredly, briefly, candidly, clearly, conceivably, consequently, evidently, (un)fortunately, frankly, (un)happily, honestly, incontestably, inevitably, luckily, mercifully, necessarily, needlessly, obviously, ordinarily, possibly, presumably, probably, rightly, simply, surely, understandably, undoubtedly*; e.g. 'This is certainly false' (= It is certain that this is false). Similar adverbial phrases are *oddly (curiously, strangely) enough, sure enough, to be sure, needless to say, of course, apart from anything else.*

The difference between adverbs like *therefore* and conjunctions like *and, but, for,* may be shown partly by the meaning ('therefore' = 'for that reason', an adverb-equivalent, §19.1), partly by the fact that conjunctions as link-words must stand at the head of a sentence or clause (e.g. 'He did me a kindness *and* I am grateful'), whereas these adverbs may stand in other positions (e.g. 'He did me a kindness; I am *therefore* grateful'). Again, in writing, sentences connected by conjunctions are usually separated only by a comma or run straight on, while sentences connected by these adverbs are separated by a semi-colon, a colon, or a full stop.

5 A clause introduced by the relative pronouns *who*, *which*, or a relative adverb such as *when* (= *and then, but then*), *whereupon*, or by such a conjunction as *though*, may be equivalent in effect to a co-ordinate sentence:

I told it to my brother, *who* [= *and he*] told it to his wife.

The whole nation was jubilant, *when* [= *but then*] like a bolt from the blue, news arrived of a serious reverse.

Whereupon [= *And thereupon*] Parliament was immediately convoked.

This may be true, *though* [= *and yet*] after all it is very doubtful.

6 When two subordinate clauses are linked together by a co-ordinating conjunction, they are *co-ordinate with one another*.

7 A subordinate clause may have another clause (or clauses) subordinate to *it*.

8 The subordination and co-ordination of clauses in a sentence may be shown in a **sentence picture,** thus (the main clause is printed in **bold type**):

> When France in wrath her giant limbs upreared,
> And with that oath which smote air, earth, and sea,
> Stamped her strong foot, and said she would be free,
> Bear witness for me how I hoped and feared.

1	**Bear witness for me**
2	| how I hoped and feared
3	| | when France in wrath her giant limbs upreared
4	| | [and] stamped her strong foot with that oath
5	| | | which smote air, earth, and sea
6	| | [and] said
7	| | she would be free.

2 *is a noun clause, object of* Bear witness (= witness *verb*) (1).

3 *is an adverb clause, adjunct of* hoped and feared (2).

4 *is an adverb clause* (*co-ordinate with* 3 *and playing the same part*).

5 *is an adjective clause, attribute of* oath (4).

6 *is an adverb clause* (*co-ordinate with* 3 *and* 4 *and playing the same part*).

7 *is a noun clause, object of* said (6).

24 General remarks on sentence analysis

1 One or more adverbial adjuncts may be found in any of the five forms of the predicate. Examples:

first form   A quiet smile played *round his lips.*
                    (adjunct of place)
                Go *when you are ready.*
                    (adjunct of time)

second form *By this time* the revolt was complete.
                    (adjunct of time)

third form   *At noon* the blackcock trims his jetty wing.—
                    (adjunct of time)   SCOTT

fourth form   He taught us Latin *regularly twice a week.*
                    (adjuncts of time)

fifth form   They made him prisoner *at once without difficulty.*
                    (adjuncts of time and of manner)

2 Note that the subject or the object or indeed any other part of the sentence may itself contain a subject, object, &c., as may be seen in the sentence picture above.

3 Vocatives and interjections, since they form no part of the subject or predicate of the sentences or clauses with which they are connected, are outside the formal structure of the sentence. Examples:

    John, be quick!   *Sir*, thou knowest.
    Where are you going to, *my pretty maid*?

A vocative may be qualified by an adjective clause, which is susceptible of analysis apart:

    O *thou* (vocative) *that tellest good tidings to Zion*, . . .

4 We may have a sentence inserted parenthetically within a sentence, with a separate structure of its own. Examples:

    He gain'd from Heav'n (*'twas all he wish'd*) a friend.—GRAY
    You say—*and I agree with you for once*—that such a course
      is impossible.

Such parenthetical sentences include: *I am sure (convinced)*, *I think, we know, I believe, I venture to say.*

5 Verbs constructed with a fixed preposition may be treated as simple verbs (see §38):

    I *waited for* (verb) him (object) a long time.

The inseparability of such construction is demonstrated by the passive: *He was waited for; It was taken stock of.*

6 Sentences of the following type present difficulties for tabular analysis:

    It is rarely *that* one of them is seen.

It was here *that* it happened.

It was on that condition *that* I went.

It is rather for books of reference *that* such treatment should be reserved.

When *is it that* you resign?

At first sight these sentences appear to be of the form of those containing a formal subject ('anticipatory *it*', §7), like 'It is right that you should go', which is the more usual way of saying 'That you should go is right'. But the sentences above will not bear this inversion; if we turn the first into 'That one of them is seen is rarely', the result is nonsense. On the contrary, they will be seen to be of the same type as:

It is Brown *that* I want.

It is you *that* I am talking to.

The man recovered of the bite,

    The dog *it was that* died!—GOLDSMITH

where 'it' = 'the person' or 'the thing', the sentences being analysed thus:

subject	predicate
It that I want	is (*verb*) Brown (*pred. noun*)

This sentence is merely an emphatic way of saying 'I want Brown—Brown and nobody else'. The emphasized word or phrase of the simple sentence is encircled within 'it is . . . that' in order to give it prominence, the simple sentence being thus turned into a complex one. When the idiom was extended from nouns and noun-equivalents to adverbs and their equivalents, the resulting sentences were such as to defy grammatical analysis— a common phenomenon when language is forced to meet as best it may the requirements of thought. The extension was natural and easy, and has no doubt been furthered by the fact that the word 'that' in English is both a conjunction and a relative pronoun. Thus in the third sentence above, while it is primarily a conjunction, it would seem to be also a relative to 'condition'.

The *that* of *It is . . . that* may be dropped:

Was it not yesterday we spoke together?—SHAKESPEARE

   'Tis distance lends enchantment to the view.—CAMPBELL

Violations of the idiomatic form *It is . . . that* are not infrequent:

   'Tis seldom *when* the bee doth leave her comb

    In the dead carrion.—SHAKESPEARE

It is at the schools and universities *where* our characters are
   moulded.

It is the poor *whom* you have always with you.

It is not of peculiar, but of general evil, *which* I am now
   complaining.—JANE AUSTEN

(*which* mechanically substituted for *that*)

   7 In sentences like the following the infinitive is probably adverbial, and therefore the italicized part will be put in the adjunct
column.

You seem *to be ill.*

He is known *to be reliable.*

The refusal was felt *to be very unkind.*

25   Schemes of analysis

Simple sentences

   1 We walked regularly before breakfast.

   2 John Gilpin was a citizen
       Of credit and renown.—COWPER

Subject	Predicate					Form of Predicate
	verb	*predicative noun adjective or pronoun*	*object*		*adjunct*	
			direct	*indirect*		
We	walked				(i) regularly (ii) before breakfast	1st
John Gilpin	was	a citizen of credit and renown				2nd
He	set		himself		(i) now (ii) to gain the royal favour	3rd
Thy eyes' shrewd tutor, that hard heart of thine	hath taught		scornful tricks	them		4th
The bigots of the iron time	had call'd	a crime	his harmless art			5th

3 He now set himself to gain the royal favour.
4 Thy eyes' shrewd tutor, that hard heart of thine,
   Hath taught them scornful tricks.—SHAKESPEARE
5 The bigots of the iron time
   Had call'd his harmless art a crime.—SCOTT

26 *Complex sentences*
Far up the lengthened lake were spied
Four darkening specks upon the tide,
That, slow enlarging on the view,
Four mann'd and masted barges grew,
And, bearing downward from Glengyle,
Steer'd full upon the lonely isle.

SCOTT

Sentence picture
A   Far up the lengthened lake were spied four darkening specks
    upon the tide
Aa that, slow enlarging on the view, four mann'd and masted
    barges grew
Ab [and] (that) bearing downward from Glengyle, steer'd full
    upon the lonely isle.

Analysis

Subject	Predicate						Form of Predicate
	verb	predicative noun adjective or pronoun	object		adjunct		
			direct	indirect			
A Four darkening specks upon the tide	were spied				(i) far (ii) up the lengthened lake		1st
Aa that slow enlarging on the view	grew	four mann'd and masted barges					2nd
Ab (that) bearing downward from Glengyle	steer'd				(i) full (ii) upon the lonely isle		1st

Analysis of the example on the following page

Subject		Predicate					Form of Predicate
		verb	predicative noun, adj. or pronoun	direct	indirect	adjunct	
A	I	had		a strong hope which never left me, that I . . . liberty			3rd
Aa	which	left		me		never	3rd
Ab	I	should¹ recover		my liberty		one day	3rd
B	I	considered		(i) myself . . . in the country (ii) that such a mis-fortune . . . to England		as to the ignominy . . for a monster	3rd
Ba	myself	to be	a perfect stranger			in the country	2nd
Bb	such a misfortune	should¹ be charged				(i) never (ii) upon me (iii) as a reproach (iv) if ever . . . Eng-land (v) since the king . . . same distress	3rd
Bb1	I		should¹ return			(i) ever (ii) to England	1st
Bb2	the king of Great Britain himself		must¹ have undergone	the same distress		in my condition	3rd

¹ Historically the infinitives with *should* and *must* are objects and the verbal groups might be so analysed, viz. *should, must* (verb) *recover*, &c. (object).

27 I had a strong hope, which never left me, that I should one day recover my liberty; and, as to the ignominy of being carried about for a monster, I considered myself to be a perfect stranger in the country, and that such a misfortune should never be charged upon me as a reproach if ever I should return to England, since the king of Great Britain himself, in my condition, must have undergone the same distress.

JONATHAN SWIFT

Sentence picture

A	I had a strong hope
Aa	| which never left me
Ab	| [*that*] I should one day recover my liberty
B	[*and*] I considered, as to the ignominy of being carried about for a monster
Ba	| myself to be a perfect stranger in the country
Bb	| [*and that*] such a misfortune should never be charged upon me as a reproach
Bb1	| [*if*] ever I should return to England
Bb2	| [*since*] the king of Great Britain himself, in my condition, must have undergone the same distress

[*For the tabular analysis of this example see previous page.*]

Syntax

28 **Syntax** means *arranging together* [Greek *syn* 'together' and *taxis* 'an arranging'] and is the name given to that part of grammar which treats of the ways in which words are arranged together in sentences and of the functions they perform.

The two parts of syntax

Syntax has to answer two questions:

1 How are meanings expressed in sentences and parts of sentences? The answer is given in Part 1 of Syntax (§§29–100), which deals with **sentence construction.**

2 What are the various meanings of words and their forms? The answer is given in Part 2 of Syntax (§§101 foll.), which deals with **meanings of forms.**

In dealing with sentence construction, those constructions which are peculiar to the complex sentence will be treated *after* those which are common to the simple and the complex sentence.

Part 1

Sentence construction

The subject

29 1 As in other languages:—

    (*a*) the subject is a noun or a noun-equivalent (§17);

    (*b*) if the subject is a declinable word, its function is shown
       by the nominative case.

In modern English, pronouns are the only words that have a
distinct form for the nominative case.

I am here. *Thou* art the man. There *he* lies.
We could hardly believe it. *Who* is at the door?
Man is mortal.

For the use of *it* as a formal and as a vague subject ('*It* is no
good crying'; 'Wasn't *it* odd, the way the baby stared at us?'),
see §7.

In sentences like 'There was a great calm', 'There rose a mighty
shout', *there* belongs theoretically to the predicate (cf. §7), but it
stands in the position generally occupied by the subject and
announces inversion of subject and verb. In French and German
we have a formal subject, *il, es*, in such circumstances: *Es
regierte ein König* 'there reigned a king'; *il sortit trois messieurs*
'there came out three gentlemen'. With formal *there* the verb
agrees in number with the noun: There *are* many difficulties;
For the first time there *are* introduced two foreign elements.

Modern English has nothing analogous to the impersonal
passive construction with a vague subject which is so common
in Latin and German; e.g. Latin *itur* 'it is gone', i.e. 'there is a
going', 'someone is going', *pugnatum est* 'it was fought', 'there
was fighting', *mihi parcitur* 'it is spared to me', i.e. 'I am spared';
German *es wird getanzt* 'it is danced', 'there is dancing'.

2 The subject is ordinarily omitted in commands and prohibitions:

> Let the cat alone.   Do not go yet.
> Stand still.

Compare, however:

> *You* go; I can't.   Mind *you* . . .

Notice also the omission of the subject 'I' in common expressions such as 'Thank you', 'Pray' (compare German *danke*, *bitte* 'thank you', 'please'), and in familiar speech: 'Who do you think has come?'—'Haven't the remotest idea'; 'Got him!'; 'Never heard of him'; 'See those black clouds?'

The predicate

The verb

30   *Agreement of the verb with the subject*

As in other languages, the finite verb agrees with the subject in number and in person. In modern English, this agreement is not now shown by difference of form except in the third person singular present indicative (*–es*, *–s*, or in archaic style sometimes *–eth*), and the second person singular present and past indicative (*–est*, *–st*; these forms are liturgical and poetical).

> The boy shout–*s* (*is* shouting). The boys shout (*are* shouting).
> I teach. Thou teach–*est*. He teach–*es*. We teach.
> He com–*eth*.

In a few verbs the forms differ considerably:

> *is:are; has:have; does:do; was:were.*

It requires care to observe the rule of agreement in longer sentences, where the wrong number is often used (especially where the subject is singular and a plural noun comes between it and the verb); e.g. 'The *appearance* of many things in the country, in the villages one passed through, and in this town, *reminds* [not *remind*] me of Dutch pictures'; '*Nothing* but dreary dykes *occurs* [not *occur*] to break the monotony of the landscape'.

31   *Construction according to sense*

A singular noun of multitude (or collective singular) may take either a singular or a plural verb according to whether collective or individual action is to be indicated. Thus:

Parliament *is* now sitting.

The crowd *has* dispersed.

Our army *was* in a sad plight.

The majority *is* thus resolved.

Three shillings *is* an excessive price.

Two-thirds of the city *lies* in ruins.

Altogether nine inches of rain *has* fallen.

In each case the 'multitude' is conceived of in the mass, as a unit. But in the following each individual of the 'multitude' is regarded as acting separately, hence the plural verb:

A majority of members *were* in favour of the plan.

A variety of suggestions *have* been made.

A number *are* going to take the risk.

The greater part of them *come* under a different head.

Youth *are* the trustees of posterity.—DISRAELI

Note also:

The military [= the soldiers] *were* called out.

The poultry [= the fowls, ducks, &c.] *are* being fed.

Note the contrast between:

There *is* heaps of jam (= *much* jam); and

There *are* heaps of plates (= *many* plates).

32 Compound subject

A compound subject is a subject made up of two or more nouns or noun-equivalents linked together by the conjunction 'and', or united in thought without a conjunction.

1 *Number of the verb*

His father and his mother *are* dead.

Fire and water *do* not agree.

The buyer and seller soon *come* to an understanding.

To them his heart, his love, his griefs *were* given.

Rule: When the subject is compound, the verb is plural.

2 *Person of the verb*

His son and I *are* friends.

You and they *would* agree on that point.

He and his brother *were* to have come.

Reason: 'His son and I' cannot be spoken of together except as 'we'; similarly 'you and they' = 'you'; 'he and his brother' = 'they'.

The verb *may* agree with the part of the subject which stands nearest to it, especially if that part serves as a climax to the whole of the subject:

One whose voice, whose look *dispenses* life and death.

Your interest, your honour, God himself *bids* you do it.

This is chiefly rhetorical or poetical, as is also the following use where the verb precedes the subject:

Therein *consists* the force, the use, and nature of language.

Formerly, where the verb preceded the subject (simple or compound) the singular form was frequent. Thus in Shakespeare:

There *is* no more such masters.

In the Bible:

Now *abideth* faith, hope, charity, these three.

For thine *is* the kingdom, and the power, and the glory.

Therein *was* written lamentations, and mourning, and woe.

When the subjects are pronouns, usage fluctuates. Thus Shakespeare has 'Thou and I *am* one', and Milton 'Both Death and I *Am* found eternal'. But Tennyson (*In Memoriam*) writes: 'Thou and I *are* one in kind'.

33 *Construction according to sense*

1 If the words composing the subject are so closely connected as to express *one idea*, the verb may be singular:

> The mind and spirit
> *Remains* invincible.—MILTON

There *was* great noise and confusion.

Law and order *was* at once restored.

The long and the short of it *is* this.

2 The preposition *with* may serve as an equivalent of *and*:

Old Sir John with half-a-dozen more *are* at the door.—

SHAKESPEARE

The side A with the sides B and C *compose* the triangle.

34 Either . . . or . . ., neither . . . nor . . .

1 These conjunctions do not link words so as to form a compound subject; the verb varies, therefore, with the number of the subjects coupled by them; e.g.

> The very rooks and daws forsake the fields,
> Where neither grub, nor root, nor earth-nut, now
> *Repays* their labour more.—COWPER

Either husband or wife *is* to blame.

Neither the French nor the Germans *desire* war.

In the first two of these sentences the verb is logically singular, and in the third it is similarly plural. Usage has, however, been irregular, as with the plural instead of the singular in the following:

Neither death nor fortune *were* sufficient to subdue the
mind of Cargill.—FOX, *History of James II*

Neither painting nor fighting *feed* men.—RUSKIN

2 When one of the subjects joined by *or* or *nor* is plural, the
verb is most conveniently put in the plural, and the plural subject
placed nearest the verb:

Neither the emperor nor his subjects *desire* war.

3 When the subjects are of different persons, the verb is normally made to agree with that nearest it:

Either my brother or I *am* going.

Neither he nor we *have* any doubt of it.

Neither you nor he *is* to blame.

Very often, however, this form of expression is awkward,
especially when the sentence is a question, e.g. '*Is* he or we
wrong?' The difficulty may be avoided by using another order:
'*Is* he wrong or *are* we?'; '*Is* he, or *are* we, wrong?' So:

Either my brother is going, or I am.

He has no doubt of it, nor have we.

You are not to blame, nor are they.

In Greek, Latin, French, German, and Spanish, when two personal
pronouns connected by conjunctions meaning 'neither . . . nor . . .' are
the subject, the verb is plural, the conjunctions being felt to be equivalent
to 'both . . . and . . . not'.

35 Predicative adjective, noun, or pronoun referring to the subject (§6)

The chief verbs that may stand in a predicate of the second
form are:—

1 verbs meaning *to be, to become, to remain, to seem, to fall:*

Be *quiet*.	The trees grew *tall*.
The lad became *rich*.	The youngsters keep *strong*.
He remains *poor*.	That comes *natural* to me.
They seem *clever*.	They went *bankrupt*.
She looked *healthy*.	He was taken *ill*.

Hiders are *good finders*.   No news is *good news*.
The whole affair has become *a nuisance*.

Who's *who*?   And that's *that*!
What's mine is *yours*, and what is yours is *mine*.—

SHAKESPEARE

Note that predicative nouns are often qualified by attributes.

Some of the verbs used in these sentences may also be used

without a predicative adjective, noun, or pronoun; they then form a predicate of the first form, either by themselves or as qualified by adverbial adjuncts: 'My father *is* no more' (=exists no longer, i.e. is dead); 'A river *was* there once upon a time'; 'Men pass away, the Universe *remains*'.

2 passives meaning *to be made, to be chosen, to be named, to be declared, to be considered, to be supposed*:

> The door has been made (*or* rendered) *secure*.
> Who has been chosen (*or* elected) *president*?
> They are thought (*or* considered) *wise*.
> The Committee is held (*or* considered) *responsible*.
> The defendant was pronounced (*or* declared) *innocent*.

3 Whether with intransitive active or with passive verbs, the predicative adjective, noun, or pronoun denotes what the subject is, was, or will be at the time of the action or as a result of the action or process:

> The snow lay *thick* on the ground.
> One sometimes feels a bit *ashamed*.
> One was rescued *alive*, but the other was found *dead*.
> The rider escaped *unhurt*.
> They all fell *sick* and died.
> He got *shaved* and *dressed*.
> We have gone *thirsty* for hours.
> The wall was built *higher*.
> I'm bored *stiff*.
> Women are marrying *younger*.
> I will live *a bachelor*.
> He turned out *a rascal*.

With many of the verbs in 1 and 2, in addition to the mere predicative adjective, noun, or pronoun, we quite as frequently have the infinitive *to be*; e.g. They seem *to be clever*. While the meaning is the same, the character of the construction is different, the adjective or noun belonging to the infinitive *to be* and not to the main verb. Compare §45.1. The infinitive is adverbial (§47).

36 *Agreement of the predicative adjective, noun, and pronoun*
1 The predicative adjective, noun, or pronoun agrees as far as possible with the word of which it is predicated (here the subject).

2 In ModE., agreement is not shown by inflexion, except in *this, these,* and *that, those*.

3 The predicative noun and predicative pronoun stand in the nominative case:

It is *I*. *Who* are they? *These* are they.

4 *It is I*. In OE. this sentence had the form 'Ic hit eom', i.e. 'I it am' = German *ich bin es* ('I am it'). In Chaucer (14th century) we find 'It am I', the predicative pronoun *it* (= the thing meant) being placed first in the sentence. Later, the *it* was taken as the subject and the verb was made to agree with it in person. Hence the modern 'It *is* I'.

'It is *me*' is frequent in current English and is used by speakers who would not say 'it's *him*', 'it's *her*', 'it's *us*', or 'it's *them*', these being generally regarded as vulgar or dialectal. The similarity of sound of *he, she,* and *we* has no doubt furthered the use of *me* as a regular and natural form. But compare French 'c'est *moi*' (emphatic form: *me* used as nominative).

5 The following adverbs have passed into adjectives capable of being used only predicatively:—

(i) of health: *well, poorly,* and (in illiterate speech) *badly* (= 'poorly'), *nicely* (as 'How's your brother?'—'Oh, he's nicely, thank you')

(ii) adverbs of the class *abed* (= 'on bed' or 'in bed'), *ablaze, about, abroad, across, afoot, agog, ajar, alight, alike, alive, aloft, apart, around, ashore, aslant, asleep, (un)aware, away, awry*

Note—Awake is of different origin, being a worn-down form of *awaken*, the old past participle of the verb *awake*.

(iii) adverbs such as *in, out, up, down, off, back, so* (= in such a state):

He is *up*. She is *down*.
They are *off*. We are *back* (*home*).
That is *so*.
To make men happy and to keep them *so*.—POPE

37   The object (§8)

1 The single object stands in the accusative case.

2 In ModE., the case is shown only in pronouns.

3 As in other languages, the object may be a noun or a noun-equivalent, with or without qualifying word. Examples:

The sound of drums aroused *me*.
Railway travelling tires *her* dreadfully.
We have been expecting *you*.
The singing pleased *us* most.
Whom were you expecting?
Fortune favours *the brave*.
I prefer *walking* to cycling. [verb-noun]

4 The object may denote:
   (i) the person to whom or thing to which something is done:
     They murdered *the king*.
     John has bought *a house*.
     The girl is picking *flowers*.
  (ii) the result of an action or process:
     The people elected *a king*.
     John has built *a house*.
     The girl paints *pictures of horses*.
 (iii) that which is done:
     I dreamed *a horrid dream*.
     He laughed *a bitter laugh*.
     The king lived *the life of an exile*.
     They are running *a race*.
     I have fought *a good fight*.—*Bible*

An object of the third kind (which denotes the action itself) is called a cognate object [Latin *cognatus* 'akin'] because it is of kindred meaning with the verb.

For *it* as an object with vague meaning, see §187.3.

The object denotes the person or thing *with respect to* which an action takes place, or it serves to point out *how far*, i.e. *to whom* or *to what* the action of the verb extends. Thus it is in origin of the nature of an adverb, or (as we say) expresses an adverbial relation. It is no longer, however, distinctly felt as an adverbial part of the sentence, but simply as denoting the person or thing that is affected. The character of the object can nevertheless change the meaning of a verb, e.g. 'She smiled her thanks'; the normal object of *smile* verb is *smile* noun ('He smiled *a bitter smile*').

5 The object may take head position when emphatic:
    A fine mess he'll make of it!
    Much good may it do him!
    Such very peculiar lives some people lead.
    That I'm afraid we can't help.

38 Verbs constructed with a fixed preposition

1 Many verbs of *intransitive* meaning, when compounded with prepositions, fixed for particular meanings, become equivalent to transitive verbs. Simple transitive verbs (often of French or Latin origin) may often be substituted for them. Thus:
    to speak to = to address

```
to call on   = to summon; visit
to laugh at  = to ridicule, deride
to wish for  = to desire
to think of  = to consider
to ask for   = to demand
to speak of  = to discuss, mention
```

So also innumerable others, such as *to answer for, to come at, to dispense with, to do with, to despair of, to look for, to put upon* (= *to impose upon*), *to rely on, to set upon, to sigh for, to tally with, to touch upon, to wait for, to wait upon,* &c.

The preposition bears no stress; e.g. *sée to it.*

2 From these must be distinguished combinations of *transitive* verbs with certain adverbs, as *away, back, forth, in, off, on, up,* &c.

Observe that the adverb in most cases may either precede or follow the object. Thus we may say: 'Call off the hounds' or 'Call the hounds off'.

Such adverbs bear stress:

Clap tó the doors.—SHAKESPEARE

Lay tó your fingers.—SHAKESPEARE

This is as a rule strongest when the adverb comes at the end: 'cáll him úp', but 'cáll up the gúard'; 'bríng the child úp', but 'bríng up the lúggage'.

The number of such combinations is practically limitless. Some of them may be themselves constructed, like simple verbs, with fixed prepositions, as *to come out with* (an expression), *to put up with, to do away with, to do out of* (slang = to deprive of), *to take up with, to live up to.*

39 *Passive construction*

1 In the passive construction of verbs taking one object, what was the object in the active becomes the subject; what was the subject in the active is generally expressed by means of the preposition *by* with the accusative.

ACTIVE	PASSIVE
A wild beast fed him.	He was fed by a wild beast.
A bullet hit him.	He was hit by a bullet.

2 When a verb with a fixed preposition (§38.1) is turned into the passive, there results a compound form consisting of the participle with the preposition remaining attached:

He was *spoken to* sharply.

Such a result cannot be *wondered at.*

I was *laughed at* by everybody.

Nobody could be *listened to* more attentively.
The proposal was *approved of.*
Don't be *imposed upon.*
He is *done for.*
It is a danger to be *striven against.*
The difference could not be *accounted for.*
A few points only are *touched upon* (or *dealt with*).
To be left till *called for.*
You heard me ill *spoken of.*

This is not restricted to verbs with *fixed* prepositions; e.g. 'The bed
had not been *slept in*'.

In the passive form the pendent preposition has light stress.
Such compounds may have *un–* prefixed to them: un-
accounted for, uncalled for, unheard of, unthought of; un-
batted at, unbickered with (Browning); untaken notice of
(Clarendon).

Verbs with fixed adverbs (§38.2) assume a similar *form* in the
passive, but the verb and adverb are to be parsed separately,
because the adverb retains its syntactical independence, as shown
by intonation and stress.

The military are being *cálled óut.*
The hounds were *cást óff.*
I was *pút úp* for the night at a farmhouse.
The cause was *táken úp* with enthusiasm.
The applicant was *sént awáy* empty-handed.

Such compounds may also, less frequently, have *un–* prefixed
to them: thus 'unhanded down' (Tennyson).

The passive construction of phrases like *come out with* is
somewhat limited; e.g. we should not say:

Such and such an expression was *come out with.*

But observe the conciseness of:

Such a state of things cannot be *put up with.*
This practice has long been *done away with.*
The plan ought to be *gone on with.*
The tragedy is *led up to* by a pathetic love-story.
He was *done out of* a thousand pounds.

40   Verbs taking an infinitive as object

The following are among the most important verbs that can
take an infinitive as object:

1 an infinitive without *to*:

I can   I must

I do   I shall
I may   I will

Of these *do*, *may*, *shall*, and *will* are in regular use as
auxiliaries of tense and of mood. Only *do* has a past participle.

With most of these verbs the objective nature of the infinitive attached
to them is for the most part not now appreciated. In the emphatic use of
will it is perhaps still to be felt, 'I will do it' meaning 'I will, intend the
doing of it', 'I purpose to do it'. (In 'He willed his own death', *will* is a
different verb.) But the original meaning of all of them shows that the
infinitive is a true object. For example *can* means primarily 'know', a
sense that survives in Chaucer's 'I can a noble tale', and 'I can French',
a use exemplified as late as the seventeenth century; 'I can swim' is
historically equivalent to Latin *scio nare*, literally 'I know to swim'. The
verb *do* is still used with the full meaning of 'perform', of which its
auxiliary function is a weakening; *may* meant originally 'to have (it) in
one's power'; *must* is the past subjunctive *mōste* (now having present
indicative force, like *ought*) of OE. **mōtan* 'to have within one's scope
or sphere', hence 'to be allowed'; from the notion of prospective or contemplated permission has been developed that of present compulsion or
obligation. *Shall* still carries vestiges of the sense of obligation (as in the
emphatic 'You shall not have it'), which is shown with full force in OE.
ic sceal 'I shall' and accounts for its use as an auxiliary of the future
tense (*I shall go* = 'I owe to go', 'I owe going'; cf. Latin *debeo ire* 'I owe,
i.e. have an obligation, am bound, to go').

2 an infinitive with *to*:

I attempt	I learn
I begin	I like
I cease	I long
I commence	I love
I continue	I mean
I decide	I ought
I desire	I prefer
I expect	I prepare
I fear	I propose
I have (= I hold as an	I purpose
obligation, hence: am	I start
bound or obliged, as	I try
'I have to go')	I used
I hope	I want
I intend	I wish
	&c.

3 *I dare* takes—

either (i) an infinitive without *to*: I dare *say*. He dare not
speak. How dare you *ask* me such a question?

or (ii) an infinitive with *to*: Will he dare *to open* his mouth?

I need takes—

either (i) an infinitive without *to*: He need not *know*. Why need he *do* it? The clothes need not *be dried*. We need not *have gone*.

or (ii) an infinitive with *to*: The clothes need *to be dried*. [or: need drying (verb-noun)] I shall scarcely need *to go*.

4 This objective infinitive must be distinguished from the adverbial infinitive: §§24.7, 158 (h).

Remark   Many of the verbs in 2 and 3 above may take other objects:

> He dared *everything*.
> She began *crying*.
> It needs *looking into*.
> The voice ceased *talking*.
> Prefer *death* to dishonour.

41   Two objects

1 'I gave him the book'. In such a sentence as this two things are mentioned as coming under the action of the verb; in other words, there are two objects. These objects are affected by the action in different ways. One of these objects, 'the book', denotes the thing which the action affects *directly*, and is called the **direct object,** and is in the accusative case like a single object; the other, 'him', takes us a step farther and denotes the person *to* or *for* whom the action of giving the book is performed; it is called the **indirect object** and is in the dative case.

Many verbs, chiefly those meaning 'offer', 'give', 'bestow', 'deliver', or 'convey' (in some way), 'show', 'tell', take two objects of this kind; the following are the most important:

I afford	I cost*
allot	deliver
allow	deny
ask	do (as 'to do the lady
award	justice')
bear (as 'She bore him	envy*
three sons')	fetch
bet*	fill
bid*	find
bring	forbid
call	forgive*
cause	gain
convey	give

I grant
  grudge
  hit (one a blow)*
  lay*
  lead (as 'She led him an
    awful life')*
  leave
  lend
  look out
  make (as 'She made us
    a curtsy')*
  offer
  owe
  pardon*
  pay
  permit*
  play (as 'to play one a
    trick')*
  prescribe
  procure
  proffer
  promise
I reach (as 'Reach me my
    hat')*
  refuse
  render
  restore
  save (as 'It saves me
    trouble')*
  sell
  send
  show
  spare*
  strike (as 'They struck the
    enemy a shrewd blow')*
  take
  teach
  tell
  throw
  wager*
  win
  wish*
  write
  yield

*With the verbs marked thus we cannot *usually* substitute an adverb-phrase formed with a preposition for the indirect object.

2 The order of objects (indirect before direct) is vital; cf. 'God send the prince a better companion!'—'God send the companion a better prince!' (Shakespeare).

3 For the simple dative with these verbs may be substituted an adverb-phrase formed with the prepositions *to* or *for*, but commonly *with an inversion in the order of the objects*; thus:

  either 1 I gave *the boy* the money
    or 2 I gave the money *to the boy*.
  either 1 He told *us* the whole story
    or 2 He told the whole story *to us*.
  either 1 Write *him* a long letter
    or 2 Write a long letter *to him*.

42 *Passive construction*

In the passive construction either the direct or the indirect object may become the subject of the passive verb; thus:

  either 1 The way was shown to me
    or 2 I was shown the way.

either 1 The post was offered (to) him
   or 2 He was offered the post.
either 1 The prize was awarded (to) them
   or 2 They were awarded the prize.
either 1 The whole story was told to my father
   or 2 My father was told the whole story.

Similarly:

He was given a cordial reception.
They were told the whole truth.
How many have been played that tune?

Sentences like (1) are found in many languages. Sentences like (2), with the 'retained object' (or 'remaining accusative', §108), are chiefly peculiar to English, but are found in Greek and occasionally in Latin.

Observe, however, that this passive construction has limits and is impossible with particular verbs or particular objects; e.g. we can say 'Something was fetched me', but scarcely 'I was fetched something'; 'A cab was called for me', but not 'I was called a cab'. On the other hand, 'The trouble was spared me' is not so natural as 'I was spared the trouble'. Possibilities are sometimes even more limited; e.g. we cannot say either 'I was cost nothing' or 'Nothing was cost me'.

Certain verbs of removal and exclusion, governing two objects, are used chiefly in the passive:

He was banished the realm. He was dismissed the service.
They have been expelled the school.

So *discharge, eject, exclude, exile, forbid.*

43 The infinitive as a second object is found with a number of verbs:

I taught him *to swim.*
Give him *to understand* that it is forbidden.
We told him *to resign.*

So *allow, permit; ask, beg, beseech, desire, entreat, pray; bid, command, exhort, order; cause, encourage, incline, induce, lead, persuade; compel, constrain, force, make; desire, prefer, wish; feel, know, observe, perceive, see; presume, understand; declare, pronounce.* See discussion of 'accusative and infinitive', §§157.3, 160.

44 Predicative adjective or noun referring to the object (§12)
1 The chief verbs which may take a predicative adjective or noun

referring to the object, are verbs denoting *to make*, *choose*, *call*, *think*, *show*—the verbs of which the passives take a predicative adjective or noun referring to the subject (§35.2):

I cannot have her made *unhappy*.
They named King John *Lackland*.
I thought the house very *low* and *dark*.
Necessity makes an honest man *a knave*.—DEFOE

2 With other transitive verbs the predicative adjective or noun may denote, as in §35.3, what the object is, was, or will be at the time of the action or as a result of the action or process:

They discovered him *hidden* in a barn.
They beat him *black* and *blue*.
They left no nook or corner *unexplored*.—POE
They kept their method *secret* (or *a secret*).
They revived metaphors gone *dead*.
The speaker soon had his hearers *cheering*.
The jury found the prisoner *guilty*.
The whole affair has become *a nuisance*.
I hope I see you *well* (cf. §36.5).
A lover's eyes will gaze an eagle *blind*.—SHAKESPEARE

45 1 Certain verbs of this class are often followed by the infinitive *to be* with a predicative noun or adjective attached to it (cf. §35.3). This entirely alters the character of the construction, as may be seen by the fact that we may often substitute for the accusative and infinitive a dependent statement introduced by *that*; e.g. I found *him to be a good scholar* (= that he was a good scholar); They know *him to be loyal* (= that he is loyal).

In these instances the predicate may be regarded as being of the third form, the italicized parts constituting the object of the sentence. On the other hand, we cannot treat a sentence like 'I took him to be a brigand' in the same way; here no *that*-clause can be substituted and the infinitive appears to be adverbial, the predicate being of the third form (with adjunct).

2 A similar ambiguity as to the form of the predicate is found with verbs of perception, as *hear*, *see*, *feel*, with which we frequently have an object followed by an infinitive (without *to*) denoting an action performed by the object:

Who saw *him die*?
No one heard *him come in*.
The prisoner felt *the snake crawl over his arm*.

These infinitives are best regarded as adverbial = 'a-dying',

&c., i.e. 'in (the act of) dying', &c. Observe that a dependent statement may not be substituted with the same meaning.

Attributes (§14)

46 Attributes are either adjectives or adjective-equivalents (§18). The present section deals with adjectives and with nouns in apposition (§18.2). For other attributes see the accusative of description (§106) and the genitive (§§111–19).

Agreement of attributes

Attributes agree as far as possible with the words which they qualify.

(1) **Adjective as attribute** An adjective that has a plural form agrees in number with the word that it qualifies.

In OE., the period of full inflexions, agreement was shown by difference of form, for gender, number, and case, just as in Latin, Greek, and German. But in ModE. there has ceased to be any *formal* change (except in *this, these, that, those*). In French there is formal agreement in gender and number.

'*These* kind of things'. Such a form of expression, in which the demonstrative adjective agrees with the (logically) 'wrong' noun, is constantly heard and occurs in good writers. In Shakespeare we have 'These kind of knaves' (*King Lear*, II ii 107).

(2) **Noun as attribute** The noun in apposition (§18) is of the same case as the word that it qualifies.

'Miss Brown'—This is an instance of a noun in apposition which is peculiar on account of the two forms which it may assume in the plural, viz. *the Misses Brown* or *the Miss Browns*. The former of these is the more proper (= the Misses having the surname Brown), but it is more natural for us to say 'the Miss Browns' without analysing the group, just as we say 'Miss Brown's'.

Adjuncts (§15)

47 Adjuncts are either adverbs or adverb-equivalents (§19). For adverb-equivalents see the genitive (§110), the accusative (§105), the dative (§§120–6), the prepositions (§§127 foll.).

Kinds of sentences

48 Sentences may be divided into four classes according to their form or the kind of meaning they express, viz.

    I STATEMENTS

II REQUESTS, i.e. COMMANDS, WISHES, CONCESSIONS
III QUESTIONS
IV EXCLAMATIONS

I Statements

49 1 Statements of matters of fact are normally expressed by means of the indicative mood:

I am happy now.   Day is dawning.
My sister sang.   She will sing tomorrow night.
She had sung before and will sing again.
Parliament was in session at the time.

2 In the present and the past tenses the compound form of the finite verb with *do, did* is employed

(*a*) with emphasis:

I do wish you would let me sleep.
Why, I do believe he is crying.
We built—when we did build—in the modern style.

This emphatic auxiliary is sometimes printed in italics.
The infinitive may precede:

He threatened to resign—and resign he did.

(*b*) without emphasis, merely as a periphrastic form:

(i) in the older language:

I do set my bow in the cloud.—*Bible*
Thus conscience does make cowards of us all.—

SHAKESPEARE

They set bread before him and he did eat.—*Bible*

The use dates from OE. times and was generally current till about 1700.

(ii) in poetry (often for metrical convenience), and in solemn or formal language:

The small birds twitter,
The lake doth glitter.

And I do nominate, institute, and appoint A.B. to be sole executor of this my will.

(iii) when there is inversion of the usual order of subject and verb, owing to the head position of part of the predicate:

Well do I remember the scene.
Bitterly did we repent our decision.

50 *Negative statements*

A statement is made negative by the use of a negative adverb or adverb-equivalent:

> I am *not* (*never*, *by no means*) happy now.
> And the subsequent proceedings interested him *no more*.—
>   BRET HARTE

But for the simple forms of the present and past indicative a compound form with *do*, *did* and the infinitive must be substituted, except with *be*, *have*, and some other verbs of one syllable like *dare*, *need*, *can*, *must*, *ought*, and all auxiliaries, and (usually) with negative adverbs other than *not*. Thus:

> He does not come now.
> My sister did not sing.
> They do not do so.

But: He has not a rag to his back.
> He never comes now.
> You dare not go.

This applies to ordinary prose; but the simple forms were formerly used in all circumstances and may still be found in poetical, archaic, or rhetorical language:

> He cometh not, she said.—TENNYSON
> Human laws reach not thoughts.

51 *Conditional statements*
Some statements speak of what *would* be done or have been done. These take the past subjunctive. Sentences of this kind are either conditional sentences of Class B (§89), or such sentences with the *if*-clause suppressed:

> She *would sing* if you asked her.
> One *could wish* it otherwise.
>   [= 'it *would* be possible for one . . .']
> I *might* perhaps *see* him now.
>   ['might' = '*should* be able']
> You *should have let* him alone.
>   [= 'it *would* have been better for you . . .']
> I *ought* not *to go*.
>   [= 'it *would* not be right for me to go']

As to the subjunctive origin of *would*, *could*, *should*, &c. in these sentences, see *anomalous verbs*, §§172 foll.

Statements like the second and third examples above may be termed **modest assertions,** i.e. cautious or hesitating statements. Modest assertions may occur in many kinds of subordinate clauses as well as in main clauses.

'He would keep repeating, Ruined! Ruined!' Such a sentence is not of this class; *would* = 'used to' and is an indicative.

II Requests, i.e. commands, wishes, concessions
52 *Commands*
(including injunctions, exhortations, instructions, suggestions, encouragements, entreaties, and warnings)

    (i) *Go* now. *Mind* what you are doing.
        You *shall go* tomorrow.
   (ii) *Let him read* it through and then *let him form* an opinion.
       Let them go [if they want to].
       They shall go [whether they want to or not].
  (iii) *Let us pray. Let us stay* here.

> *Sing we* merrily unto God our strength.—*Psalm* lxxxi
> *Climb we* not too high,
>   Lest we should fall too low.—COLERIDGE

Commands are expressed

(i) in the second person by the imperative or by *shall* with the infinitive.

In colloquial language an emphatic request is often conveyed by *do* with the infinitive: *Do take* some more. *Do go*, please. In similar conditions a personal pronoun is sometimes used with the imperative: *You leave* that dog alone; Out *you go*.

The imperative may be lost by ellipsis: Quick! Down! Here! Out of the way!

The command may sometimes take the form of a question: *Will you be* quiet? (= *Be* quiet).

See also §92.

(ii) in the third person by the imperative *let* with the infinitive (in a predicate of the fourth form) or by *shall* with the infinitive.

(iii) in the first person by the imperative *let* with the infinitive (in a predicate of the fourth form). This construction is limited in the first person *singular* to such expressions as 'Let me see' and to poetry.

Sentences like 'Let me (us, him, her, them) go' may mean either (*a*) 'allow me (us, him, her, them) to go', with *let* as main verb, or (*b*) 'I (we) will *or* resolve to go', 'he (she, they) may *or* should go', with *let* as auxiliary. Most occurrences are (logically) susceptible of either interpretation; cf., however, unambiguously (*a*) 'Let me be'; 'Please let me have my ticket'; 'Let me tell you'; unambiguously (*b*) 'What about going for a walk? Yes, let's'; 'Let there be light'. The second meaning was in earlier English expressed by the subjunctive; cf. the examples in small type in (iii) above.

53 *Prohibitions* (*negative commands*)

Prohibitions are expressed

(i) in the first and third persons as in commands, with the addition of a negative adverb.

(ii) in the second person by a compound form, *do* with the infinitive, the negative *not* standing between them; e.g. *Do not go; Don't be fooled.*

This is the regular prose construction, but in poetry and solemn speech we often have the simple form: '*Tell* me *not* in mournful numbers . . .'; also when the negative adverb is *never*, as '*Never complain* and *never explain*' (Disraeli); '*Never you mind.*'

Let is an imperative; a negative command in the first person (in the simple form: 'Let us not go', with *not* qualifying the infinitive) may therefore be constructed also, as in the second person, less formally with *do*: Don't let's go.

54 *Wishes*

1 Formal or solemn wishes for the *future* or the *present* are commonly expressed by *may* with the infinitive:

Long *may* she *reign*!

The simple subjunctive mood survives chiefly in a few traditional blessings and imprecations and in archaic language:

Heaven *forbid*!

(God) *bless* you!

So *help* me God!

Peace *be* with you.

It survives also in trivial usage, as 'Grammar *be* hanged!'

2 Wishes for the *present*, i.e. that something were otherwise than it actually is, were expressed by *Would* (*that*) or *Oh that* with the past subjunctive:

Would (*that*) I *were* there!⎫
Oh that I *were* there! ⎬[but I am not]
Would (*that*) (*Oh that*) it *were* not so! [but it is]

3 Wishes for the *past*, i.e. that something had been otherwise than it actually was, were expressed by *Would* (*that*) or *Oh that* with the past perfect subjunctive:

Would (*that*) (*Oh that*) I *had* never seen it!

Would in these expressions is for *I would*, and is itself a subjunctive = 'should wish'.

When *Oh* stands alone as introducing word, the verb *precedes* the subject: *Oh were* I there!

4 A wish involving the first person may be expressed by *Oh* with the infinitive preceded by *to*: '*Oh to be* nothing, nothing!' or by *Oh for* . . .: '*Oh for* a closer walk with God' (Cowper).

5 The *if*-clause of a conditional sentence of Class B (§89)—the main clause being suppressed—is sometimes equivalent to an expression of wish: *If it were only true!*

6 Elliptical wishes may omit the verb: *Good luck to you! More power to your elbow!*

The uses in 2, 3, 4 above are confined to the higher literary language.

55 *Concessions*

Concessions are expressed by the subjunctive:

> *Be* it so.
>
> He would go, *happen* what might. (complex sentence with noun-clause as subject = Let |whatever might [happen]| happen)

But an ordinary statement may have concessive force: *He may talk a great deal*, but there is nothing much in what he says.

In 'I will go, *be the weather what it may*', '*Cost what it might*, he would have it', we have formally two sentences, the one a statement, and the other a concession equivalent in force to a general relative clause: 'whatever the weather may be', 'whatever it might cost'.

III Questions

56 As in other languages, questions fall into two classes:

1 Class A: questions that can be answered with 'yes' or 'no'. These are expressed by inverting the order of the subject and the verb of the corresponding statement; e.g. '*You are* right' becomes '*Are you* right?' Examples:

> Have you a penny?
>
> Was he ready?
>
> Are you sleeping? Have you forgotten?—TENNYSON
>
> Would she sing if you asked her?
>
> (complex sentence containing an adverb clause)
>
> Is not (Isn't) your brother happy? *or*
>
> Is your brother not happy?
>
> Do cats eat bats? Do bats eat cats?—CARROLL

The (elliptical) inversion, indicating a question, may follow a statement in normal order: 'You are there, *are you*?' Negation may appear either in the statement or in the question: a negative in the question supposes the answer 'yes': 'You can walk, *can't you*?'; a negative in the statement supposes the answer 'no': 'You can't walk, *can you*?'

2 Class B: questions that cannot be answered with 'yes' or 'no'. These are introduced by interrogative pronouns, adjectives, or adverbs (*wh*-words), with inversion of subject and verb, except where the introducing word is the subject of the question. Examples:

> Who goes there?
> What have we here?
> What was the cause of this sudden change?
> Which is the way?   What does he say?
> Where is the prince?
> Where are you from?
> Why should they know their fate?

3 The use of the different forms of the present and past indicative active is the same as in negative statements (§50):

> Had you a right to do that?
> Doesn't he ever mention it?
> How do you do?
> Need you stay?
> Can't you go?

4 Some statements may be converted into questions in which surprise or incredulity is expressed, by altering the tone of voice in which they are spoken, or (in writing) by means of the mark of interrogation:

> You are not going yet?
> They told you that?

5 Questions as to what *is* or *was to be done*, sometimes called deliberative questions, often express the verbal idea by the infinitive or bare stem of the verb:

> I *honour* thee?
> Why *trouble* to read it?

The sense of 'I honour thee?' is 'Am I to honour thee?' or 'To think of my honouring thee!' The second paraphrase shows the affinity of some questions of this kind to the exclamation. It is not surprising, therefore, that in the well-known passage of *Macbeth* (I vii 59)

> If we should fail?—*We fail?*

many editors read 'We fail!' i.e. as an exclamation.

IV Exclamations

57 1 Exclamatory statements, i.e. those expressing emotion, are usually marked either by a special introductory word or by inversion of subject and verb or of other parts, accompanied by a mark of exclamation:

> How spotless the snow is!
> How short the days are!
> How well he might have done!

A sentence in the form of a question, wish, or command is often exclamatory: Could one have believed it! Don't I hope so! Oh for a moment's rest! Be quiet and sit down! Stop!

2 Many exclamatory sentences are elliptical (cf. §4), a frequent form consisting of a noun qualified by an attribute; they may consist of single words as the relics of sentences possible or imaginary:

> How foolish of him!
> What a task!
> That awful dream!
> Poor dog!
> Peace! Silence!

Sentences introduced by an exclamatory infinitive are usually of this character; e.g. 'To think of your coming to Oxford and not letting me know!' Compare the exclamatory intonation of deliberative questions (§56.5): 'What are we to say?'

When exclamations involve the first person singular or plural we have often 'me' not 'I', or 'us' not 'we' (cf. the Latin accusative of exclamation):

> Dear *me*! Poor *us*!

3 Simple interjections express sudden emotions: Ha! ha! ho! ho! he! he!

Under this head may be grouped the few survivals of this class of word, viz. *ah ha*, *oh*, *hi*, and expressions of laughter, as well as the interjectional use of sacred names and their deformations, such as *gosh*, *golly*, *lor'*, *law*, &c.

The complex sentence (§20)

Noun clauses (§22)

58 Noun clauses fall into two great classes:

A Those that express **that** something *is* (*was*, *will* or *would be*, *has* or *had been*) or **that** something *shall* or *should be*.

(i) I know that you are just.

Such sentences are in origin two co-ordinate sentences:

You are just: I know *that* (demonstrative pronoun: cf. the identity of German *das* and *dass*, pronoun and conjunction, distinguished by spelling).

Here the *that*-clause contains a statement of fact, and is called a **dependent statement.**

(ii) I command $\begin{cases} \text{that you should act justly.} \\ (less \ commonly) \ \text{that you act justly.} \end{cases}$

This also is the product of two co-ordinate sentences:

You should act justly: I command *that*.

Here the *that*-clause expresses what *should be*, and is called a **dependent command** (= clause of desire).

The *should* in these clauses had originally independent meaning and was equivalent to 'ought', but that meaning became weakened and now it stands as a subjunctive-equivalent.

B Those which are introduced by an interrogative or exclamatory word:

(i) Tell me what you said = Tell me: What said you?

I ask whether it is fair = I ask: whether it is fair (or not)?

Here the subordinate clause is interrogative and is called a **dependent question.** Note that the sentence as a whole is not a question but a statement; a dependent question may be defined as *a question clause in a complex sentence*, or *a noun clause introduced by an interrogative word*.

The verb on which a question clause depends need not be a verb of 'asking'; e.g. I do not know whether you are just = I do not know the answer to the question 'Are you just?'

(ii)   It is strange how unjust you can be

= It is strange: How unjust you can be!

Here the subordinate clause is exclamatory and is called a **dependent exclamation,** the sentence as a whole being a statement.

A noun clause may play the part of:

1 subject: *That you are unjust* is clear. (Or with formal subject *it*: It is clear *that you are unjust*)

2 object: I declare *that you are unjust*.

3 a predicative noun, or a noun in apposition to a noun or pronoun in the main clause:

My hope is *that you will not be unjust*.

The fact *that he is a traitor* is well known.

See to it *that you are not unjust.*

Sometimes the *that*-clause may be regarded as being in apposition to a pronoun implied in the main clause:

I am glad *that you have not been unjust.* (Cf. I am glad *of this.*)

59 A Dependent statements and dependent commands

The following constructions are used:

1 *that* with a verb in the same mood as in the corresponding independent sentence, but with adjustment of tense if necessary (see §153):

I confess *(that) I am wrong.*

He was afraid *(that) he would be ill.*

It happened *(that) he had just come.*

2 *that* (or, with some verbs, *lest*) with the subjunctive or a subjunctive-equivalent (usually formed with *shall, should,* in certain circumstances with *may, might*):

I insist *(that) he be allowed his freedom.*

We ordered *that he should be released.*

We fear *lest worse may be in store for us.*

Lest is now somewhat formal or affected. *That* is frequently omitted.

3 an accusative and infinitive:

That proved *me to be right.*

He declared *himself to be a true subject.*

Bid *me do anything for you.*

Tell *him to go.*

How these constructions are used in connexion with particular verbs, adjectives, &c. is shown in the following sections.

60 *Verbs of 'saying', 'thinking', 'perceiving', 'knowing', and 'showing'*

1 These verbs take either (*a*) *that* (often omitted) with a finite verb:

I tell you *(that) you are mistaken.*

He denied *(that) he had done it.*

The telegram says *(that) he is on his way.*

They have confessed *(that) they are in the wrong.*

Do you think *(that) you could manage it?*

I believe *(that) we shall have rain.*

You will see *(that) the prisoner is innocent.*

I know *(that) I should not be successful.*

It was proved *that this could not have happened.*
[Here we have a formal subject, §7]
That such an event might happen cannot be disputed.
or (*b*) an accusative and infinitive, except 'say', 'tell', and a few
others:

Everyone declared (reported, believed, knew, supposed,
concluded, presumed, assumed) *him to be innocent.*
Few have thought (proved, shown) *themselves to be worthy
of the honour.*
I took *him to be one who had been shipwrecked like myself.*

Early ModE. usage was much freer; e.g. Izaak Walton (1653)
writes: Bacon observes *the pike to be the longest-lived* of any
freshwater fish.

2 Equivalent expressions like the following take a *that*-clause
only: adjectives—(I am) *sure, certain,* &c.; (it is) *certain, clear,
manifest,* &c.; nouns—(there is a) *rumour, certainty, doubt,* (the)
knowledge, thought, proof, &c.; (on the) *ground, condition,
understanding, supposition,* &c.:

It was clear *that he had no chance.*
The thought *that he might miss the train* was galling.
These were unmistakable proofs *that he had been there.*

3 The verb TO DOUBT in an interrogative or negative sentence
may take *but that* or (simply) *but,* with the same meaning as
the ordinary *that:*

I do not doubt *but that you are surprised.*
Who doubted *but the catastrophe was over?*

This construction with *but that* or *but what* was formerly
much commoner than now (when it is only in literary use and
somewhat archaic), and accompanied *to make no question* and
similar expressions. So: 'We did not know *but that* (*what*) he
might be ill'; 'I'm not sure *but what* I agree with you'.

4 The verbs TO HOPE and TO EXPECT, from the nature of their
meaning, take a future or a future-equivalent in the *that*-clause:

I expect (or hope) *we shall come.*

We may sometimes have *should* with the infinitive as a subjunctive-equivalent in present time:

Providence furnishes materials, but expects *that we **should**
work them up ourselves.*

The accusative and infinitive may be used as an equivalent
construction:

I expect *you to join us* (= *that you will join us*).

When the subject of both main and subordinate clauses is the same, the infinitive (with *to*) may be used as an equivalent:

I hope *to come* = I hope *(that) I shall come.*

They expected *to be victorious* = They expected *(that) they would be victorious.*

'Expect' in the loose sense of 'suppose' may be followed by any kind of *that*-clause:

I expect *he is (was, will be, would be) away.*

61 *Impersonal verbs of 'happening' and 'seeming'*

These verbs take a *that*-clause (as in §60):

It happened *that I was away at the time.*

[formal subject, §7]

It seems *that you had forgotten me.*

It appears *that he had been ill.*

These sentences cannot, however, be reversed: we may say: 'That he has been ill is likely enough', but not: 'That he has been ill it appears'.

Equivalent expressions: nouns—(it is a) *fact*; (there is a) *probability, likelihood,* &c.; adjectives—(it is) *probable, likely*:

There is every probability *that the government will be defeated.*

It is likely *that they will never return.*

The same idea may be expressed also by the use of a preposition with the gerund: 'There is every probability *of the government being defeated'.*

62 *Verbs of 'rejoicing', 'grieving', 'wondering', 'complaining'*

These verbs take a *that*-clause (as in §60):

I rejoiced *that I had won a victory.*

Many were surprised *that he was not elected.*

He complained *that he had been badly treated.*

But where the speaker contemplates the *thought* of something happening or having happened rather than the mere fact of its happening, the *that*-clause takes *should*; for instance—

I grieved *that you* **should** *be so angry.*

In Latin in these instances we have the accusative and infinitive or *quod* with the subjunctive (as opposed to *quod* with the indicative); in French *que* with the subjunctive (as opposed to *de ce que* = 'at the *fact* that' with the indicative).

The above verbs are not so common as expressions of equivalent or kindred meaning; e.g. nouns—(it is a) *pity, piece of good fortune, good thing, misfortune,* &c.; adjectives—(I am) *glad,*

sorry, grieved, angry, annoyed, surprised, &c.; (it is) *strange,
wonderful, fortunate, unfortunate*, &c.:

> We are glad *that you are able to come.*
>
> She is annoyed *that you are going.*
>
> *That he has acted thus* is a great misfortune, but *that he
> **should** have acted thus* is not surprising.
>
> It is not strange *that his admiration for those writers **should**
> have been unbounded.*

The same idea may be expressed also by the use of a preposition
with the gerund: 'I rejoiced *at his having won a victory'*.

63 *Impersonal expressions denoting 'it is right', 'it is wrong',
'it is necessary', and* (in negative and interrogative sentences)
'it is possible'

These expressions take a *that*-clause with the subjunctive, or
much more commonly, an equivalent, with *should; that* may
often be omitted:

> It is right ⎫
> It is not right ⎬ (*that*) *you* **should** *be dismissed.*
> Is it right? ⎭
>
> Is it possible (*that*) *he* **should** *be so foolish*?
>
> It is good *that a young man* **bear** *the yoke in his youth.*—
> *Bible*
>
> It is time *we left.*
>
> It is time *he got married.*

But where 'is it possible?' expresses surprise at something
having happened, the indicative is used:

> Is it possible *that he has left England*?

Equivalent

A common equivalent of the *that*-clause is 'for' governing an
accusative and infinitive:

> It is wrong *for you to do this* (= *that you should do this*).
>
> It is impossible *for one to be angry with him.*
>
> What could be better than *for you to go*?

So with expressions of kindred meaning:

> There is every reason *for him to be displeased.*

64 The verb TO FEAR and equivalent expressions take *that* or
lest followed by the future, or *may* (*might*) with the infinitive:

> We ⎧ fear ⎫ *lest* ⎫ we ⎧ *may* ⎫ *be led astray.*
>   ⎨ feared ⎬ or ⎬   ⎨ *might* ⎬
>   ⎩   ⎭ *that* ⎭   ⎩   ⎭

There was every risk *that we might fail.*

In these sentences the fear relates to the future; a fear almost amounting to an anxious conviction that something *is, was,* or *will be* the case is expressed with a *that*-clause as in §60:

We fear *the news is* (*will turn out to be*) *only too true.*

I am afraid *I shall be late.*

I am afraid *I was cross.*

65 *Verbs and expressions implying an act of the will*

With these the *that*-clause may assume one of three forms:

1 The subjunctive may be used, but it is now restricted to formal and rhetorical language except to express an unfulfilled wish (which requires the *past* subjunctive, §54.2):

It is requested *that this part of the ticket* **be** *retained during the evening.*

The Lord Chancellor put the motion *that the House* **go** *into Committee on the Education Bill.*

Christian love requires *that we* **overlook** *our neighbour's wrongs to us.*

We urge that *he* **be** *allowed a free hand.*

I wish *he* **were** *here.*

2 A subjunctive-equivalent with *shall* (*should*) is more usual:

It is proposed   ⎫ *that Parliament* **shall** *allow a*
There is a proposal ⎭   *company to be formed.*

He commanded   ⎫
We gave orders   ⎬ *that no one* **should** *move.*
Orders were given ⎭

3 In ordinary speech the indicative is most common with expressions meaning 'take care', and some others:

Mind *he* **does** *not see you.*

He took care *that his work* **was** *correct.*

You will see *it* **doesn't** *get lost.*

66 *Equivalent*

With many verbs of this class the accusative and infinitive is a common construction (cf. §96.1):

I must ask *you to go away.*

They forced *me to get down.*

I had in vain entreated *them not to meddle with the egg.*

67 B Dependent questions and dependent exclamations (§58B)

The **introducing words** are: *who* (*whom, whose*), *what, which; where, whither, whence, when, how; whether, if* (= whether).

It is necessary to distinguish between dependent questions and relative clauses introduced by *what*; e.g. 'Ask him *what he has done*'; 'The missionary described exactly *what he saw*'. In the latter instance the *what* may be replaced by 'that which', in the former it cannot: that is the general test.

It is sometimes difficult, however, to tell whether a particular clause as written is a dependent question or a relative clause; e.g. 'I told him *what I had told you*'. Does this mean 'I answered his question as to what I told you', or 'The same that I told you, I told him'? Observe that the meaning of the sentence depends upon intonation. N.B. In Latin the choice of pronoun and mood would determine the character of the clause: *Dixi ei quid tibi dixissem* (dependent question); *Dixi ei quod tibi dixeram* (relative clause: here we might also have *id quod* 'that which').

68   The dependent question or exclamation has the same mood as the corresponding independent question or exclamation, but its tense is commonly adjusted to the time of the verb in the main clause:

I now tell you *why it is so.*
> Corresponding independent question: *Why is it so?*
In past time: I then told you *why it was so.*

The dependent clause is often in front position. Examples:
> Natural selection decides *who shall live.*
> I wonder *whether it is true.*
> They asked me *why I sat so still.*
> I don't see *why they don't become full members.*
> *Why he should have thought all this* we cannot imagine.
> *What results it can have* we cannot yet tell.
> We were deliberating *whether we should cross.*
> > Corresponding independent question: *Shall we cross?*
Therefore *should* is indicative = 'were to'.

69   When the dependent question is deliberative, i.e. expresses what *is to be* done, and its subject may be unambiguously inferred from the main clause, the infinitive with *to* is a common construction:

Tell *me what to do.* [= what I am to do]
I do not know *where to go.* [= where I am to go]

It depends also upon the nature of the main verb whether this equivalent may be used; e.g. we can say 'They knew where to go', but not 'They thought where to go'.

Reported speech
70 Two methods may be employed in reporting:

1 The reporter may **quote** words or views in their original **independent** form; this is called **direct speech** or **oratio recta**:

'We do not think of going,' they said, 'till the winter sets in.'

2 The reporter may use the form of a clause, or clauses, **dependent** on a verb of *saying, thinking, writing,* &c., called the **leading verb;** this is called **indirect speech** or **oratio obliqua**:

They say that they do not think of going till the winter sets in.
They said that they did not think of going till the winter set in.

DIRECT SPEECH	INDIRECT SPEECH
'To adopt the young man's suggestion *will*,' he said, 'make no real difference except in detail. Two troops *may* as well be sent out as one. The Phelatahs *have* always been false; and *I have* found that the nettle *did* not sting yesterday, or today, for the first time; as far as *my* poor experience *goes* back, it *has* always been a stinging plant; and, as far as *my* poor discernment *foresees*, it always *will* be. *Remember* the proverb "that if judgement *belongs* to the old, quickness of perception *belongs* to the young"; or, to speak in the language of the people, that the young foal of the ass *may* have a better sight than the father of lions. *Have we* not noticed that even the prejudices of the vulgar *are* often based upon something substantial, which chiefs of high lineage *may* not have condescended to observe? *Does* not the weasel in its own small circuit see more clearly than the bison, which *relies*	'To adopt the young man's suggestion *would*,' he said, 'make no real difference except in detail. Two troops *might* as well be sent out as one. The Phelatahs *had* always been false; and *he had* found that the nettle *did* not sting yesterday, or today, for the first time; as far as *his* poor experience *went* back, it *had* always been a stinging plant; and, as far as *his* poor discernment *foresaw*, it always *would* be. *Let them remember* (or *They should remember*) the proverb "that if judgement *belonged* (or *belongs*) to the old, quickness of perception *belonged* (or *belongs*) to the young"; or, to speak in the language of the people, that the young foal of the ass *might* (or *may*) have a better sight than the father of lions. *Had they* not noticed that even the prejudices of the vulgar *were* often based upon something substantial, which chiefs of high lineage *might* not have condescended to observe? *Did*

upon its force, and not upon its sharpness of vision? (or *Does*) not the weasel in its own small circuit see more clearly than the bison, which *relied* (or *relies*) upon its force, and not upon its sharpness of vision?

In a word, *I advise you* not to discard a prudent suggestion from whatever source it *may* come, and *my* vote *will* be heartily given in favour of *this* young man who *has* just withdrawn from *your* presence, and to whom *I should* be more inclined to listen from the fact that he *must* have imbibed some of the wisdom of his uncle, the great chief of the East.' In a word, *he advised them* not to discard a prudent suggestion from whatever source it *might* come, and *his* vote *would* be heartily given in favour of *that* young man who *had* just withdrawn from *their* presence, and to whom *he would* be more inclined to listen from the fact that he *must* have imbibed some of the wisdom of his uncle, the great chief of the East.'

71 The way to convert oratio recta into oratio obliqua is shown in the following tables.

	Oratio recta		Oratio obliqua

1 Tense

	present	becomes	past
	perfect	,,	pluperfect
	future	,,	secondary future
	future perfect	,,	secondary future perfect

If the reporter desires to make a statement of the speaker's his own, he will retain the tenses of the O.R.

2 Pronouns and **possessive adjectives** are all put into the third person; e.g. *I*, *me*, *my* become respectively *he*, *him*, *his;* *you*, *your*, *yours*, being either singular or plural, become *he*, *him*, *she*, *her*, or *they*, *them*, *his* or *their*, *his* or *theirs*.

Note—The paucity of English pronouns of the third person (for instance *he*), as compared with Latin *hic*, *is*, *ille*, *iste*, *ipse*, *se*, often requires the insertion of explanations in brackets to make it clear who is referred to. See the example in §72.4.

3 Adverbs and **this**

	here	becomes	there
	now	,,	then
	this, these	,,	that, those

72 *The above conditions apply when the leading verb is of the third person and in the past tense.* This is the form of O.O. with which we are best acquainted, but it is obvious that various other forms are possible. We may consider the following example:

(1) Croesus, king of the Lydians, said to Solon the Athenian: My Athenian guest, *your* great fame *has* reached even to *us*, as well of *your* wisdom as of *your* travels, how that as a philosopher *you have* travelled through various countries for the purpose of observation. *I am* therefore desirous of asking *you* a question. *Tell me* who *is* the most happy man *you have* ever seen.

If Croesus reported this speech, he would say:

(2) I said to Solon that *his* great fame *had* reached even to *us*, as well of *his* wisdom as of *his* travels, how that as a philosopher *he had* travelled through various countries for the purpose of observation. *I was* therefore desirous of asking *him* a question. *I asked him to tell me* (or *Would he tell me?*) who *was* the most happy man *he had* ever seen.

['Would he tell me?' represents a possible 'Will you tell me?' of the oratio recta.]

If Solon reported the speech, he would say:

(3) Croesus told me that *my* great fame *had* reached even to *them*, as well of *my* wisdom as of *my* travels, how that as a philosopher *I had* travelled through various countries for the purpose of observation. *He was* therefore desirous of asking *me* a question. *He asked me to tell him* (or *Would I tell him?*) who *was* the most happy man *I had* ever seen.

If a third person, not a Lydian or an Athenian, reported, he would say:

(4) Croesus, king of the Lydians, said to Solon, the Athenian, that *his* (Solon's) great fame *had* reached even to *them* (the Lydians), as well of *his* wisdom as of *his* travels, how that as a philosopher *he had* travelled through various countries for the purpose of observation. *He* (Croesus) *was* therefore desirous of asking *him* (Solon) a question. *Would he tell him*, who *was* the most happy man *he had* ever seen?

Adjective clauses (§22)

73 Adjective clauses are introduced by relative pronouns (*who, what, which, whoever, whatever, whichever, that, as*), relative adjectives (*which, what, whichever, whatever*), or relative adverbs (*when, where, whereat, whereby, wherein, whereof, whereon,* *whereupon, how, why, as*), referring to a noun or noun-equivalent called the antecedent, expressed or implied in the main clause.

The words *when, where, as* may be called relative adverbs when they define or identify an antecedent expressed or implied in the main clause; e.g. 'at a time *when* (= at which)', 'a little village *where* (= at or in which)', 'in the same way *as* (= in which) you did before'. In such instances, the time, place, or manner is already fixed in the *main* clause, as in the above examples by *at a time, a village, the same*, and the subordinate clause is merely an adjectival qualification of these expressions. Where, however, the *subordinate* clause fixes the time, place, or manner of the action of the main clause, *when, where,* and *as* are conjunctions (such an adverb clause may, however, in older usage be *resumed* by a correlative adverb in the main clause, e.g. 'Wheresoever the carcass is, *there* will the eagles be gathered together'). For examples, see §§81–2.

A practical test is given by the fact that *an adjective clause introduced by* when, where, *or* as *cannot precede the entire main clause, whereas an adverb clause so introduced may do so.*

74 Agreement of the relative The relative agrees as far as possible in gender, number, and person with its antecedent; but its case depends on the part it plays (as subject, object, &c.) in its own clause.

Who is the only relative that is declinable (accusative *whom*, genitive *whose*).

> The man *who* (or *that*) *wrote this book* is now famous.
> He *who praises everybody* praises nobody.—JOHNSON
> The day, *which opened brightly*, closed with a violent storm.
> The people *whom* (or *that*) *we saw* were Nihilists.
> Edison is an inventor *whose fame is world-wide*.
> This is the same dog *that we saw yesterday*.
> Bees like the same odours *as we do*.

Examples with relative adverbs are:

> I know a bank *where the wild thyme blows*.—SHAKESPEARE
> It was a time *when sedition was rife*.

In sentences like 'There's Mr Jones, *who* they declare is the richest man about here', the relative is sometimes treated as if it were the object of 'declare', *whom* being substituted for *who*; whereas in fact the relative is the subject of 'is', and 'they declare' is a parenthetical sentence inserted in the midst of the relative clause. But we may change the construction and make 'declare' the verb of the relative clause having an accusative and infinitive dependent on it; thus: 'There's Mr J., *whom* they declare *to be* the richest man . . .'

Conversely, avoid the nominative in such a sentence as 'They were a people *whom* it was not perfectly safe to attack', where the relative is the object of the infinitive 'to attack'. Test the correctness of your sentence by inverting the order thus: 'to attack whom was not perfectly safe'—a possible form of the clause, but awkward.

75 Agreement of the verb of the relative clause   The verb agrees in number and person with the relative when this is the subject of the clause:

> I, *who* **understand** *your reasons*, will support you.
>
> O Thou *who* **art** *our sure defence* . . .
>
> It is you *who* **are** *to blame*.

Non-observance of proper concord is frequent in sentences like the following:

> That is one of the few good books *that* **have** *been written on the subject.* [the antecedent is *books*, not *one*: therefore *have*, not *has*]

76 Two kinds of relative clauses

Relative clauses may be used for two purposes:

(*a*) where the clause is subordinate in sense, to help to limit or define more clearly the antecedent, which without the relative clause would in some instances make no sense, and in others convey quite a different sense from that intended:

> This is the house *that Jack built*.
>
> Uneasy lies the head *that wears a crown*.

In such instances the relative clause is introduced by *that*, except after a preposition or where *whose* is required; no comma is used to separate the relative clause from its antecedent; and the relative may be omitted in the usual way (see below §77).

This kind of clause is mostly used where the antecedent is presented as belonging to a class, and is hence naturally found after a superlative or after a restricting pronoun or adjective like *all*, *some*, *any*, *the*, *no*, &c.:

> All *that live* must die.
>
> He is the greatest historian (*that*) *we have ever had*.
>
> These are some of the cases (*that*) *I have noticed*.
>
> Adrian IV was the only Englishman *that was ever Pope*.

(b) where the clause is co-ordinate in sense, to give some additional information about an antecedent which is already sufficiently defined:

A brother of his, *who has a candle factory*, is rolling in riches.

These books, *which are only a small part of my collection*, I picked up in France.

I gave him a shilling, *which was all I had with me*.

In such instances the relative clause must be introduced by *who* (*whom*), *which*; a comma separates the relative from its antecedent; and the relative cannot be omitted.

In general, the relative pronoun is equivalent to a conjunction + a demonstrative or personal pronoun: *who* = *and* (or *but*) *he, she; which* = *and* (or *but*) *it, that,* &c. In fact, in the spoken language, these co-ordinating forms are often preferred, which makes the number of sentences of class (b) considerably smaller than those of class (a). The co-ordinating nature of the relative comes out very clearly when *which* refers to a whole sentence (see *Relatives*, §194.5). But in the written language the need of discrimination between the two classes described is often felt, and the non-observance of the distinction is liable to lead to misunderstanding. Example: 'All the members of the Council, who were also members of the Education Board, were to assemble in the Board-room'. This would naturally imply that all members of the Council were members of the Education Board. 'That', instead of 'who', would clearly express the meaning intended, which is that 'those who were members of the Education Board as well as of the Council were to assemble'. If we retain *who*, the omission of the comma after 'Council' is sufficient, *who* then referring, in accordance with general practice, to persons (see below).

Observe the significance of the distinction in the following: 'In two of the instances, *which* have actually come under my notice, the system has worked well'; 'In two of the instances *that* have actually come under my notice the system has worked well'. The first means: 'Two of the instances have come under my notice; in those instances the system has worked well'. The second means: 'Instances have come under my notice; in two of these the system has worked well'.*

---

*It may be noted that, in speech, *which* might be used in either case, and the sense would be quite adequately conveyed by the intonation and rhythm of the sentence.

The tendency to appropriate *who* and *which* to persons and things respectively often outweighs other considerations; thus 'People *who* live in glass houses' is usually preferred to 'people *that*'; this is particularly so with *those, they,* and other pronouns of common gender, as also with *he* and *she*. 'Those *who* are in favour of this motion' is more usual than 'those *that*'.

The following passages show the two uses occurring side by side with no difference of meaning:

> Render therefore unto Caesar *the things which are Caesar's*; and unto God *the things that are God's.—Bible*

> For just experience tells, in every soil,
> That *those who think* must govern *those that toil.—*
> GOLDSMITH

77 Absence of the relative In modern English prose the relative pronoun is omitted, generally speaking, only when it is the object of the clause. In speech the tendency is to omit the relative as much as possible, and to prefer (e.g.) 'the book I am reading' to 'the book that I am reading'. In the written language its omission is often felt to be undignified.

But the relative is also omitted when it is the subject of its clause:

(i) in colloquial language, after *there is, it is, who, what is?*:

> There was a woman *called this afternoon.*

> There's somebody *wants to see you.*

> It's an ill wind *blows nobody any good.*

> Who was that *went by*? [This avoids saying 'that that' or 'that who'.]

Compare:

> There is no power in Venice
> *Can alter a decree established.—*SHAKESPEARE

(ii) in poetry and in the older language, without restriction:

> What words are these *have fallen from me*?—TENNYSON

> I know a charm *shall make thee meek and tame.—*SHELLEY

> These Londoners have got a gibberish with them *would confound a gipsy.—*SHERIDAN

> I have a brother *is condemned to die.—*SHAKESPEARE

Adverbial *that* (or *which* following a preposition) is very often understood:

> Look at the way [*that (in which)*] he tackled the job.

> I shall go back *the way I came* [*by the way that (by which) I came*].

He was out *the day I called* [*on the day that* (*on which*) *I called*].

Omission of the relative *that* enables us to couple constructions involving different cases of the relative, e.g. 'For all we have and are' (Kipling), where the *that* which is not expressed is (i) accusative objective and (ii) predicative pronoun. This, however, is felt to be a licence.

Omission of the antecedent is much less common, and chiefly poetical:

To help *who want*, to forward *who excel*—POPE
He helped to bury *whom he helped to starve*.—POPE

i.e. *those who, those whom*.
The following lines are noteworthy:

There is a book *who runs may read*,
Which heavenly truth imparts—KEBLE
(= There is a book *which he* who runs may read, *and* which . . .

Such a construction occasionally leads to the **attraction** of the relative into the case of the omitted antecedent:

Vengeance is his or *whose he sole appoints*.—MILTON
[*whose* = *his whom*]

Conversely the antecedent may be attracted into the case of the omitted relative (**inverse attraction**):

When him *we serve's* away—SHAKESPEARE
[*him* = *he whom*]

For the various uses of relatives, see §§193–5.

78   Moods in relative clauses   As in other languages, the verb in relative clauses may be in any mood or tense which is possible in main clauses; but—

(*a*) *ever*-clauses (general relative clauses), i.e. those introduced by *whoever, whatever, whichever*, &c., especially when the action is to be marked as prospective, take the subjunctive (now normally possible only with *be*), or more commonly *may* (*might*), *shall* (*should*) with the infinitive:

Whatever the cause **be,** the author has hardly done justice to his subject.
Whatever its other merits **be,** that is not one of them.
Whatever you **may** *say*, I shall not change my opinion.
However much he **might** *try*, he could not succeed.

But the indicative (without adjustment of tense) is used with the same meaning:

Whatever he does, let it be prompt.

(*b*) Relative clauses with final or consecutive meaning sometimes take *shall* (*should*), equivalent to the Latin subjunctive:

Build me straight . . . a goodly vessel
That **shall** *laugh at all disaster*.—LONGFELLOW

An act might be passed *that* **should** *not entirely condemn the practice*.

[In the last sentence *did* instead of *should* would be less formal.]

A common equivalent of such an adjective clause is the infinitive:

He had nothing *to say* [= that he should say, Latin *quod diceret*].

I am not the man *to be frightened by such a threat* [= who should be frightened, Latin *qui terrear*].

Note also:

There is every reason *why* (= for which) *he* **should** *be displeased*. [Equiv. *for his being displeased*]

79 An *if-* or *though*-clause subordinated to the relative adverb *as* takes the past subjunctive:

The stones did rattle underneath

As if Cheapside **were** *mad*. [i.e. *as they would rattle if C. were mad*]

You look *as if you* **had** *been frightened*.

They argue *as if* (*though*) *the matter* **were** *doubtful*.

He felt *as if he* **were** *being suffocated*.

Adverb clauses (§22)

80 Adverb clauses are classified according to the adverbial meaning that they express. Thus there are adverb clauses of—

(*a*) **Time,** introduced by
when, **whenever,* †*whensoever,* †*what time*
while, whilst, †*the while* (*that*)
after, before, †*ere,* †*or ever*
until, till
since
as (with *as soon,* †*soon, as long, so long, as often* in the main clause)
than (dependent upon *no sooner . . .* in the main clause)
immediately, directly (†*that*)
now (*that*), *once* (†*that*)

(*b*) **Place,** introduced by
where, **wherever, wheresoever*
whence, *whencesoever
whither, *whithersoever

(*c*) **Reason,** introduced by
because
since
as, that (with correlative or connective expressions in the main clause)
†*for that*

in that
seeing that
in as much as
whereas
considering (*that*)
why
how

(*d*) **Purpose,** introduced by
that (depending on *in order*,
to the end, *so*)
lest (= *that . . . not*)

(*e*) **Result,** introduced by
that (with correlative *so*,
such)

(*f*) **Condition,** introduced by
if (†*if that*), †*an*, †*and*, †*an
if*, †*if so be that*
unless (= *if . . . not*)
whether . . . or (= *if . . . or
if*)
that (depending on *in case*,

*on condition, supposing,
provided*, all of which may
be used without *that*)
†*except*, †*but*, †*so*, †*save*
(*that*)
so (*as*) *long as*

(*g*) **Concession,** introduced by
though, although
even if, even though
†*albeit*, †*howbeit* (*that*)
for all (*that*)
notwithstanding that

(*h*) **Comparison,** introduced by
as (with *so, such, as* in the
main clause)
than
the (with *the* in the main
clause)
as if
as though

*Words marked thus are also used to introduce relative clauses (§73).
†Expressions marked thus are obsolete or archaic.

Adverbial clauses of various but not of all kinds may be abridged by the omission of features not essential to the meaning: 'How to be happy *though married*' [i.e. though one is married]; 'When only in his fifth year . . .' [i.e. when he was . . .]. Such contracted subordinate clauses began to be frequent in the later years of the sixteenth century.

81   *Temporal clauses* (*clauses of time* §80a)
Temporal clauses group themselves mainly under three heads:
   1 The largest group comprises those which speak of a matter of fact in present or past time. These take the indicative mood:

When it is fine, I go for a walk.
It was broad day *when he awoke*.
They waited *till the ship sailed*.
It is some time *since I saw such acting*.
The natives fled *as soon as they saw us*.
Now (*that*) *you are here*, you had better stay.
A telegram came *after you had gone*.

2 But if the action of the temporal clause is prospective (i.e. if the temporal clause refers to the future, whether from a present or past point of view), three constructions are possible:

(*a*) The subjunctive mood may be employed, though in ModE. this is chiefly limited to poetry and higher prose:

> The tree will wither *long before it* **fall.**—BYRON
> I cannot do anything *till thou* **be** *come thither.*—*Bible*
> There is full liberty of feasting from this present hour of five *till the bell* **have** *told eleven.*—SHAKESPEARE

(*b*) A commoner construction, however, is *shall* or *should* with the infinitive. This *shall* or *should* is used in all three persons and both numbers (*when I shall, when you shall, when he shall*), and is to be regarded as forming a subjunctive-equivalent and not as a mere future tense; thus it corresponds closely to the Latin and Greek subjunctive which is so common in prospective clauses. Note that *shall* stands in present time (i.e. when the main clause contains a verb of present time), *should* in past time (i.e. when the main clause contains a verb of past time):

> I am waiting *until he* **shall return.**
> He determined to wait by the roadside *until it* **should be** *dark.*

(*c*) But the commonest construction in modern English prose is the indicative mood, and especially in present time. We do not now say 'I am waiting *till he come*' or 'I am waiting *till he shall come*', but 'I am waiting *till he* **comes**'.

This use of the present indicative referring to future time is a characteristic feature of the Germanic languages, which have no proper future tense but only a future-equivalent (see §142); just as we may say 'he starts tomorrow' for 'he will start tomorrow', so we say 'when he starts' for 'when he shall start'.*

> Keep them *till he* **sends** *for them.*
> *When I* **get** *the letter*, you shall have it.

The corresponding use of the past indicative for *should* with the infinitive is less common, but by no means infrequent:

> He determined to resign *before the crash* **came.**
> [in formal style: *should come*]
> I should go ahead quickly *when once I* **started** [or *had started*].

---

*This use of the present indicative is therefore to be regarded as a peculiarity of tense and not as a subjunctive-equivalent.

Similarly we say: 'I shall go ahead when once I *have started*' (*have* for *shall have*); 'I should have gone ahead when once I *had started*' (*had* for *should have*). Cf. §146.2.

3 *Ever*-clauses of time (i.e. clauses introduced by *whenever*) take the same moods and tenses as other temporal clauses: '*Whenever it is fine*, I go for a walk'; '*Whenever he fell asleep*, he had horrible dreams' (like the examples under 1 above); '*Whenever I start*, I shall go ahead' (like the examples under 2 above).

In colloquial language *ever* may serve merely to indicate that the action of the main clause follows immediately on that of the temporal clause, and does not express a general statement, as: 'You may come as soon as *ever* you are ready'. In Scotland 'whenever', which in England means 'as often as', is used in the sense of 'as soon as (ever)'; e.g. 'I shall go out *whenever* I have had my dinner' = '*as soon as* I have had my dinner'.

82 *Local clauses* (*clauses of place* §80b)
Like temporal clauses, local clauses fall under three heads:

1 Local clauses which speak of a matter of fact in present or past time take the indicative mood:

The house stood *where three roads met*.
Remain *where you are*.
Go back *whence you came*. In colloquial style: Go back (*to*) *where you came from*.

2 But if the action of the local clause is prospective, two constructions are possible:

(*a*) We may have a subjunctive-equivalent, *shall* or *should* with the infinitive:
Where the tree shall fall, there it shall lie.

(*b*) But the usual construction is the plain indicative as in the corresponding class of temporal clauses (§81.2c):
Where the tree **falls,** there it shall lie.

3 *Ever*-clauses of place (i.e. clauses introduced by *wherever, wheresoever, whithersoever*) take the same moods and tenses as other local clauses: '*Wherever he happens to be*, he is on the point of going somewhere else'; '*Wherever she went*, there would he' (like the examples in 1); '*Wherever you are*, do your duty' (like the example in 2). But where the local clause is prospective in present time we often have *may* as a subjunctive-equivalent; e.g.

Do your duty *wherever you may be.*
Might is also correspondingly found in past time:
He did his duty *wherever he might be.*

83 *Causal clauses (clauses of reason §80c)*
The mood in causal clauses is unrestricted:
As you are not ready, we must go without you.
He will succeed *because he is in earnest.*
Since you insist on it, I will consider the matter again.
Conjunction-equivalents are in use of the following kinds:
(*a*) a phrase formed with a preposition governing a noun with a *that*-clause in apposition, as *on the ground that, for the reason that. Because* = 'by (the) cause', which was often followed by *that*, is of this origin. (See §60.2.)
(*b*) a verb-adjective governing a *that*-clause as object, as *seeing that, considering that* (see §100.3).
(*c*) a preposition governing a *that*-clause, as *in that.*

84 *Final clauses (clauses of purpose §80d)*
1 Final clauses introduced by *that* take *may* with the infinitive in present and future time, *might* in past time:
I eat *that I may live.*
They climbed higher (so) *that they might get a better view.*
2 Negative final clauses are sometimes introduced by *lest* = *that . . . not*), which takes *should* with the infinitive:
I eat *lest I should die.*
Climb we not too high,
Lest we should fall too low.—COLERIDGE
3 The subjunctive, the original mood in OE., has survived in archaic and poetical use. The use of *may* and *might* as sub-junctive-equivalents goes back to OE. times.
To act that each tomorrow
Find us farther than to-day.—LONGFELLOW

85 *The infinitive of purpose*
When the subject of the final clause denotes the same person or thing as the subject of the main clause, purpose is often expressed by the infinitive with *to* or *in order to*:
I come *to bury* Caesar, not *to praise* him.—SHAKESPEARE
We must go early *in order to get* a good place.
For . . . to may also be used to indicate an intended result:
For a word to have a meaning, it must stand for something.

For everything to turn out right, you must plan in advance.
In this instance, however, the subject need not be the same in
both parts of the sentence.

86 *Consecutive clauses* (*clauses of result* §80e)
1 Result is expressed by *that* with the indicative or by *as* linked
to the infinitive with *to*:

He was so weak *that he fell down several times.*
It is so simple *that a child can understand it.*
He is so lame *that he cannot walk.*
He is so lame *as to be unable to walk.*
I spoke so *that everyone could hear.*
I spoke so *as to be heard by everyone.*
Be so good *as to come.*
The pain is such *that he cannot sleep.*

2 *That* with the indicative denotes *fact,* and can be used only
when the result is *actual.* *As* with the infinitive does not necessarily denote fact, but may be used in all circumstances; it *must*
be used when the result is to be marked as merely *contemplated*
or *in prospect.* The subject of the infinitive, unexpressed, must be
the same as that of the main verb.

3 *So* or *such* is usually present in the main clause.

87 If-*clauses* (*clauses of condition* §80f)
A complex sentence consisting of an adverb clause of condition
(the *if*-clause, called the protasis) and a main clause (called the
apodosis), which states a result of the condition, is called a
conditional sentence.

Such sentences fall into two main classes, which are distinguished by the form and meaning of the **main clause:**

A Those in which the main clause does not speak of what
would be or *would have been,* and the *if*-clause implies nothing
as to the fact or fulfilment (**open condition**); e.g. 'If you are right,
I am wrong'; 'If the sky falls, we shall catch larks'. (The *if*-clause
does not imply that you actually *are* right, or that the sky
actually *will* fall.)

B Those in which the main clause speaks of what *would be*
or *would have been,* and the *if*-clause *implies a negative* (**rejected
condition**); e.g. 'If wishes were horses, beggars would ride'
[implication: wishes are *not* horses]; 'If the sky were to fall, we
should catch larks' [implication: the sky does not fall].

Class **B** has a **special conditional form** in English as in other languages: the main clause is expressed by a 'should' or 'would' (past subjunctive), the *if*-clause is marked by a special use of tenses and moods to indicate the *remoteness* of the supposition; e.g. 'If you *were* right, I *should be* wrong'.

88   *Class A*

1 When the main clause does not speak of what *would be* or *would have been*, the *if*-clause takes the indicative:

    a **present time** *If this is true*, that is false.

                    If he says that, he is wrong.

    b **past time**   *If he said that*, he was wrong.

    c **future time**   *If he says that*, he will be wrong [*says* = 'shall say'].

2 In the above sentences, the time referred to is the same in both clauses; but this is not necessary:

    If he did it, he is a fool. (past and present)

    If he is wise, he will come. (present and future)

    If you have done so, you will be ruined. (perfect and future)

3 A main clause which does not speak of what *would be* or *would have been* is free, i.e. it may assume any of the forms of the simple sentence (§§49–57):

    If you know, tell us. (command)

    If you have tears, prepare to shed them now.—SHAKESPEARE
    (command)

    May I die *if I know*! (exclamation)

4 The main clause may suffer ellipsis; e.g. 'Well, if it isn't old Aunt Jane!' The *if*-clause is often reduced to essentials; e.g. 'Stay with us, *if only for a few moments*' [= if you stay . . .].

The *if*-clause of a sentence like 'If he *is* ready, he will come' is ambiguous; *is* may be either a true present or a future-equivalent (§146.2); it may mean either 'If he is ready now' or 'If he shall be ready in the future'. There is the same ambiguity in French and German. See below (§89, Add. rem.), and cf. §89.3.

89   *Class B*

1 When the main clause speaks of what *would be* or *would have been*, both clauses take the subjunctive,* as in Latin and German:

---

    *The subjunctive is not always distinguishable in form; but there is no justification for not calling *had, did, would* subjunctives in the above sentences. They are historically so, and their identity in form with the corresponding indicatives is accidental (contrast *were* as distinct from *was*). Moreover, they cannot be past indicatives because they do not refer to past time.

a **present time**
  If he **said** *that,* he **would** be wrong.
  Were *my brave son at home,* he **would** not suffer this [i.e. *if my brave son were at home* . . .].
b **past time**
  If he **had** *said that,* he **would** have been wrong.
  Had *we gone,* we **should** have let you know.
c **future time**
  If he **were** *to say that* ⎫
  If he **said** *that*   ⎬ he **would** be wrong.
                                 ⎭

Where the time referred to in both clauses is the same we have:

	In the if-*clause*	*In the main clause*
a	past subjunctive	*should* or *would* with present infinitive
b	pluperfect subjunctive	*should* or *would* with perfect infinitive
c	*were to* with present infinitive	*should* or *would* with present infinitive

2 The time referred to, however, need not be the same in the two clauses. An *if*-clause referring to past time may be joined to a main clause referring to present time:

  I *should be* better off now if I *had taken* your advice.

3 The past subjunctive may refer either to present or to future time; hence a sentence like '*If he said that,* he would be wrong' is ambiguous, and may belong to either *a* or *c*, because 'said' = either 'were saying now' or 'were to say in the future'. The same ambiguity exists in French and German. Compare the exactly similar case in §88.3.

4 Command is excluded from main clauses of this class.

5 Note that the past subjunctives 'had' (= 'would have') and 'were' (= 'would be') are used only archaically in the main clause:

  If thou hadst been there, my brother *had* not died.—*Bible*
  Were the world now as it was the sixth day, there *were* yet a chaos.—SIR THOMAS BROWNE

6 The main clause may suffer ellipsis; e.g. 'If he only knew what he wanted!' An *if*-clause, by ellipsis of a main clause of undetermined or imaginary form, is frequently used to express a wish that is impossible or unlikely of fulfilment; e.g. 'If only an unbreakable button could be attached to an unbreakable thread!'

ADDITIONAL REMARKS

1 In *if*-clauses of Class A, English, German, Latin, and French all employ the indicative mood (e.g. 'If he *is* ill, he cannot go'), just as they do ordinarily in other adverb clauses ('When he is ill', 'Because he is ill', &c.). All tenses may be used, and without any peculiarity, except that the present not infrequently refers to future time.

	Present time	*Past time*	*Future time*
English	if he is	if he was	if he is (= shall be)
German	wenn er ist	wenn er war	wenn er ist (= sein wird)
Latin	sī est	sī erat	sī erit
French	s'il est	s'il était	s'il est (= sera)

2 In sentences of Class A there is no implication about the fulfilment of the condition: they are colourless. When I say 'If you can convince me of this, then I confess myself wholly in the wrong', 'If it has thundered, it has also lightened', I do not mean to imply that you *can* convince me of this, or that it *has* thundered.

It is true that we may use 'if' when the context shows that a *fact* is in our minds. '*If thy family is proud*, mine, sir, is worthy' = 'Thy family is no doubt proud, but mine is worthy'. '*If Elizabeth was resolute for peace*, England was resolute for war'. This is frequent with shortened *if*-clauses, as 'He is fifty years old *if a day*'. Or again, the conditional sentence *as a whole* may suggest that the speaker does not believe the supposition to be true; e.g. 'If this is so, I'm a Dutchman'; 'Do it if you dare'. But in all these instances the *if*-clause itself suggests nothing as to the actual state of the case; any implication of reality or unreality that the sentence contains is due to the sentence as a whole or to the context.

3 In clauses of Class B the *if*-clause presents two peculiarities:
(i) In all the languages considered above, a *readjustment of tense* takes place, the action of the verb being *thrown back* in time.
(ii) In English, German, and Latin there is also a *readjustment of mood* (*subjunctive for indicative*), but usually not in French.

	Present time	*Past time*	*Future time*
English	if he were	if he had been	if he were to be
German	wenn er wäre	wenn er gewesen wäre	wenn er wäre
Latin	sī esset	sī fuisset	sī sit
French	s'il était	s'il avait été (s'il eût été)	s'il était

90 *Class C*

There is a third class of conditional sentences in which the main clause is like that of Class A (i.e. does not speak of what *would be* or *would have been*), but the *if*-clause marks the action as merely *contemplated* or *in prospect* or implies a certain *reserve* on the part of the speaker.

> If this *be* so, we are all at fault.
>> [*Be* implies 'I do not say (or know) that it is'.]
>
> *Should* you desire an interview, I shall not refuse to meet you.
>
> If thou *read* this, O Caesar, thou mayst live.—SHAKESPEARE
>
> If it *were* so, it was a grievous fault.—SHAKESPEARE
>> [*Were* implies 'I do not say (or know) that it was'.]

1 The *if*-clause has the subjunctive or (in future time) its equivalent, *should* with the infinitive.

2 The present subjunctive refers to present or to future time.

3 The past subjunctive refers both to past and to future time. (Cf. §89.3.)

The type is now chiefly in rhetorical or formal literary use.

91 *Modes of introducing if-clauses*

1 'If' and 'unless' (= 'if not') are the commonest conjunctions employed to introduce *if*-clauses.

'If' was often followed by 'that' in the older language. 'An', a worn-down form of 'and' (and commonly so spelt in Shakespeare's time), was once a common introducing word = 'if'. 'Except' and 'but (if)' were formerly frequent in the sense 'unless'.

> *If that* her breath will mist or stain the stone,
> Why, then she lives.—SHAKESPEARE
> No more of that, Hal, *an* thou lovest me.—SHAKESPEARE
> I will not let thee go, *except* thou bless me.—*Bible*
> For every wight of hir manere
> Might cacche ynogh, *if that* he wolde,
> *If* he had eyen hir to beholde.—CHAUCER

2 An *if*-clause in Class B (or C) is sometimes expressed, as in German, by a simple inversion of subject and verb without a conjunction:

> Were I = If I were   Had I = If I had
> *Should it be wet*, I shall stay at home.

3 Alternative clauses of condition are introduced by 'whether . . . or' (= 'if . . . or if').

4 The following are often used as equivalents of a conditional conjunction—

(i) 'provided (that)' = 'if only', 'supposing (that)', 'in case', 'on condition (that)'. The first two of these phrases may be employed to introduce any class of *if*-clause; the last two in clauses implying a reserve (Class C), in which class all four may take the subjunctive or indicative without appreciable difference of meaning:

>I give my consent, *provided that he goes immediately*. (Class A or C)
>
>*Supposing it happens*, what shall you do? (Class A or C)
>
>*Supposing it happened*, what should you do? (Class B)
>
>*Supposing he is not at home*, what then? (Class A)
>
>They were always ready *in case they should be wanted*. (Class C)

(ii) 'So long as' in colloquial style has sometimes the meaning 'if only':

>You won't fall *so long as you hold on tight*.

The older language used 'so' in this sense; e.g. 'Let them hate me *so they fear me*'; 'I am content *so thou wilt have it so*'.

5 The *if*-clause is frequently elliptical and consists only of the conjunction and an essential word or phrase:

>*If necessary*, we must go elsewhere.
>   [i.e. *If it is necessary*]
>*Whether good or evil*, you will have to put up with it.
>   [i.e. *Whether it is* or *be good or evil*]

So: 'if so', 'if not', 'if ever', 'if anyone', 'if anywhere'.

92   *Equivalents of an* if-*clause*

Two co-ordinate sentences, connected or not by a conjunction, the first of which is a command or a concession and the second a statement, may be equivalent to a conditional sentence:

>*Lose your nerve* and you are finished.
>
>*Take care of the sense* and the sounds will take care of themselves.
>
>*Do it* or it will be the worse for you. (= If you don't do it . . .)

A phrase used absolutely may also be equivalent:

>*Rain or no rain*, holiday-makers are setting out.
>
>There will be stoppages, *bridge or no bridge*.

93   *Concessive clauses* (§80g)

1 In concessive clauses which imply a fact the verb is in the indicative mood:

Although they are rich, ⎫
Rich though they are, ⎬ they are not happy.
Rich as they are, ⎭

Though he talks a great deal, there is not much in what he
    says.

Few though they were, the English fought desperately.

Much as schools of linguistics differ, they have this much in
    common.

A predicative noun or adjective (and occasionally an object)
may come first in the clause.

2 In concessive clauses which refer to future time (whether
from a present or a past point of view) or in which the action is
contemplated or in prospect, it is common to use the subjunctive
mood, or in recent times its equivalent *should* with the infinitive.
The indicative, however, is often employed without any appreciable difference of meaning.

Though everyone **desert (should desert, deserts)** you, I will
    not.

Even if he **should** *fail this time,* he can try again.

3 There is a class of concessive clause, formerly common but
now of limited range, in which the verb in the subjunctive comes
first. This is now used chiefly with the present tense and in
sentences like the following, where the subject of the subjunctive
has a relative clause attached:

We cannot receive him, **be** *he who he may.*

It must be done, **cost** *what it may.* [i.e. let it cost what it
    may cost]

Compare, however, also:

Try as he may, he will never succeed.

She could never play well, *try as she would.*

The word-order may be accounted for by the fact that the
clause has retained the form of the independent sentence (*Be it
what it may* = 'let it be what it may') and indeed is still felt to
have a certain independent character.

94 *Equivalents of a concessive clause*

Where the subjects of the main and the concessive clauses are
identical, the concessive clause may become elliptical and shrink
down to the conjunction and the essential word or phrase of the
clause. Thus *though, although,* with a noun, adjective, or adverb
(or their equivalents) are frequent equivalents of a concessive
clause (cf. §91.5):

His critics, *though outvoted*, have not been silenced.
Though no fighter, he is not a coward.
It is unfortunate, *though very natural*.

95 *Comparative clauses* (§80h)
Clauses of comparison are of two main kinds. They are free in respect of mood and tense.
  1 Where the clause is introduced by *than* depending on a word denoting comparison (usually an adjective or an adverb):
    There was a bigger gathering *than had been usual for many years*.
    You will find these dates taste better *than they look* [i.e. than what they look to be].
    The young of today are always wanting to be somewhere else *than where they are*.
    More know Tom Fool *than Tom Fool knows*.
  2 Where both main and subordinate clauses contain correlatives, viz. *so . . . as . . ., as . . . as . . ., the . . . the . . .*
    This is as wise a plan *as the other was foolish*.
    It is not so easy *as you think* [i.e. as you think it is, think it to be].
    The more learned a man is, the more modest he is.
  3 A comparative clause is often contracted by leaving only sufficient of it to indicate that with which the comparison is made; the case of a noun or pronoun following *than* or *as* in such circumstances depends on the verb that may be supplied:
    You cannot dislike them *more than I* [i.e. more than I do].
    It concerns you as much *as me* [i.e. as it concerns me].
  4 Both clauses may be highly elliptical, especially in colloquial or proverbial language:
    The more the merrier [i.e. the more we are in number the merrier we shall be].
    The sooner the better.
    The nearer the bone, the sweeter the meat.

96 A contracted comparative clause may contain a clause subordinated to itself; thus we may have a *that-*, *if-*, or *though-*clause subordinated to *as* or *than*.
  1 A *that*-clause subordinated to *than* takes the subjunctive or more commonly its equivalent, *should* with the infinitive:
    I desire nothing more *than that you* **should** *come*.
    Rather *than (that) he* **should** *suffer*, I will go myself.

The type of such sentences is found in the first example given; it is elliptical for 'I desire nothing more than I desire that you should come'. The construction has thence been extended to other instances, as in the second example. Note the use of the infinitive as an equivalent for the *that*-clause: 'I desire nothing more than *for you to come*', 'Rather than *let* him suffer, I will go myself'. Cf. §§63, 65–6. Impersonal verbs are frequent: 'It lasted longer than was expected' [i.e. than it was expected that it would last].

2 An *if*-clause subordinated to *as* or *than* takes the past subjunctive:

I am much happier *than if I* **were** *rich.*
I am not so happy *as if I* **were** *at home.*

97 He is too wise *to do this.*
This is equivalent in meaning to a sentence containing a comparative clause, as may be shown by the way in which the idea is expressed in other languages: German 'Er ist zu klug, als dass er dies täte' (= too wise *than* that he should do this); Latin 'Prudentior est quam ut hoc faciat' (= he is wiser *than* that he should do this). But, in form, the English sentence is a simple one, and the infinitive must be taken as an adverbial adjunct to *wise*, expressing the extent of the person's wisdom. French has a similar construction: 'Il est trop prudent *pour faire ceci*'.

LIKE as a conjunction—The use of *like* as a conjunction = *as*, e.g. '*like* I do', '*like* he was', 'the sun was setting just *like* it is now', is frequent as a loose colloquialism, but is avoided by careful speakers and writers. Historically it is shortened from *like as*, e.g. '*Like as* a father pitieth his children, so the Lord pitieth them that fear him'—*Bible.* (The word *like* here properly belongs to the main clause, and is an adverb = 'in like manner': *As* a father pitieth his children, so *in like manner* the Lord pitieth them that fear him.)

98 *Variants and equivalents of the absolute clause*
Absolute clauses are clauses in which the predicate is formed with a participle instead of a finite verb, and which are equivalent in meaning to adverb clauses of time, reason, condition, or concession, or to an adverbial phrase expressing attendant circumstance. Such a group is called 'absolute' [Latin *absolutus* = free], because in construction it is felt to be free of the rest of the sentence.

1 In modern English, the case of the absolute clause is the nominative (**nominative absolute**), as is evident when a pronoun is the subject of the clause:

This done, we went home. [i.e. *When this was done:* **clause of time**]

The ice being thus broken, everyone became almost aggressively reminiscent.

It being very cold, we made a fire. [i.e. *Because it was very cold:* **clause of reason**]

She failing in her promise, I have been diverting my chagrin. —SHERIDAN

I will come, *weather permitting*. [i.e. *if weather permits:* **clause of condition**]

A meeting will be held, *God willing*, next week.

Away go the two vehicles, *horses galloping, boys cheering, horns playing loud*. [i.e. with horses galloping, &c.: **attendant circumstance**]

2 The absolute clause is often elliptical by the omission of the participle:

The ceremony over, the crowd dispersed.
Sword in hand, he faced his foe.
The meeting took place, *A.B. in the chair*.

3 In general prose, spoken or written, the absolute participial construction is almost limited to conventional phrases like 'weather permitting', 'God willing', 'all being well', 'things being as they are', 'other things being equal', 'that being so'.

In some types of literary language it is similarly to a great extent restricted to set phrases like 'this done', 'there being (no objection)', 'it being (shown)', 'such being the case', 'regard being had to . . .', and other formulas with *being* or *having*, as '*The tenants being away*, the house was locked up', or with past participles, as 'The same might be said of many families, *our own included*'; '*All things considered*, we have been successful'. Examples of the kind contained in the following sentence are rarely found outside the language of books: '*Allowance being made for the inconsistencies referred to*, the book is a valuable contribution to the subject'.

But poetical usage has been freer, as in '*We sitting*, as I said, the cock crew loud' (Tennyson).

4 The equivalent of an absolute clause exemplified in the following quotation is rare and poetical:

How can ye chant ye little birds,
   And I sae fu' o' care?—BURNS

But in illiterate language there is a similar construction with the accusative: 'How could the room be cleaned, *and me with my rheumatism*?'

99 A participle which has no subject of reference in the sentence, or which, if referred to its grammatical subject, makes nonsense, is not uncommon when a writer intends to use the absolute construction.

> *Calling upon him last summer*, he kindly offered to give me his copy. [Say: *When I called . . .*]
>
> *Being stolen*, the Bank of England refused to honour the note. [Say: *It being stolen*, or better: *The note being stolen*, the Bank of England refused to honour it.]
>
> *Having left daughters only*, the property was sold for the immense sum of £135,000.—BOSWELL, 1765. [Say: *He* or *she having left . . .*]
>
> *Looking out for a theme*, several crossed his mind. [Who was looking out? Not 'several', certainly.]

The only instance in which it is unambiguous to omit the subject in an absolute clause, is when the unexpressed subject is indefinite (= one, people).

> *Taking* everything into consideration, our lot is not a happy one. [*Taking* = one taking, i.e. if one takes]
>
> *Counting* (or *Including*) ourselves, ten persons went. [*Counting* = if one counts]
>
> Nearly the whole of the work of a laundry is done *standing*. These prayers are to be said *kneeling*. [= the people kneeling]

So 'generally (humanly) speaking', 'allowing for . . .', 'judging by . . .', 'assuming . . .', 'talking (speaking) of . . .', 'given time'.

How such instances as these have been further developed is shown in §100.3(i).

The absolute construction seems in all periods to have been felt to be foreign to the genius of English, and consequently usage has considerably fluctuated (e.g. in the case employed), while its use has often given rise to vagueness and confusion of expression.

100 **Historical note on the absolute participial construction**
1 In English, as in other languages, the participial adverb clause is in origin essentially an adverbial adjunct consisting of a noun or noun-equivalent in an oblique case with a participle in agreement with it, and denoting an attendant circumstance, cause, or condition. In OE. the participial group was put in the dative case; thus '*ēow slǣpendum* forstǣlon hīe thone līchaman' = 'for you sleeping, they stole away the body', i.e. 'while you slept'. Compare Latin '*urbe captā* rediit domum' = 'with the city taken, he returned home', i.e. 'the city having been taken', 'when, as, *or* since the city was taken'. In course of time the case-meaning in English became obscured, with the loss of inflexions, and the group assumed the

form of a clause with a subject in the nominative case and a predicate containing a participle, equivalent in meaning to an adverbial clause but having no formal link with the main clause.

2 The construction is distinctly alien to English. In OE. it appears as a direct imitation of the Latin ablative absolute, and in ME. it is mainly due to French, Italian, and classical influence. In Wyclif's translation of the Bible, for example, the Latin construction is simply imitated, e.g. John viii 30: *Hym spekynge* this thingis [= Vulgate: haec *illo loquente*] manye bileveden into him. In Chaucer we find chiefly French and Italian influence at work. When we come to Sir Thomas Malory (about 1480) we find the construction fully developed with the nominative case, but it is infrequent. (Example: There came into his halle, he syttynge in his throne ryal, xij auncyen men.) In early ModE. its use is extensive only with classicists, but in Shakespeare and the Elizabethan dramatists generally it is very frequent and in a great variety of forms, many of which would be impossible now. (See Shakespeare, Tp. v i 100, 2H6 i i 167, H8 ii i 42, Cym. ii iv 7, All'sW. v iii 47, R2 i iii 259.) Restoration times saw the construction naturalized and made a part of the syntax of the language. (Milton's *me overthrown, him destroyed, us dispossessed* are mere Latinisms.) Clarendon uses it frequently in his *History of the Rebellion*, and in his narrative style it has often obvious advantages over the ordinary clause-form.

3 In the absolute construction have originated certain expressions which are equivalent to prepositions or conjunctions. They have arisen in three different ways:

(i) From an active participle with a vague subject implied (as 'one', 'people' = French *on*). Of this kind are *barring, considering, excepting, including, regarding, respecting, seeing, touching*. When certain of these are used to govern whole clauses, they perform the work of a conjunction.

Seeing (that) you are here, you may as well stay.

Here *seeing* may be paraphrased as 'when one sees'.

(ii) From an active participle having a noun (or noun-equivalent) in agreement. To this class belong the prepositions *during, pending, notwithstanding*. Of these, *during* and *pending* are the English adaptations of French *durant* and *pendant*, which were frequently used in the absolute construction *cela durant* = 'this during *or* lasting', *ce pendant* = 'this pending *or* awaiting decision' (now written as one word *cependant*, and meaning 'however'). These phrases might equally be written *durant cela, pendant cela*, which led subsequently to the participles being regarded as prepositions, and it is as such that they function in modern French. The history of their English representatives is exactly similar.

Notwithstanding is directly modelled on the French *nonobstant*, which has a prepositional use only, while by ellipsis of object *notwithstanding* has come to be a sentence-adverb also. Observe that we may still say *this notwithstanding*, preserving the old form and order of the participial construction.

(iii) From a passive participle with a noun (a noun-equivalent) in agreement. To this class belong *except* and *provided*. *Except* is taken from French *excepté; cela excepté* (= that excepted) gave 'except this', just as *cela durant* gave 'during this'. The change in the grammatical character of *except* probably began before the 16th century; it may possibly have been felt sometimes as an imperative, in the same way that *bar* is now, 'two to one bar one'. Like some of class (i), *except* may also govern a whole clause and thus form a conjunction-equivalent. *Provided*, representing French *pourvu*, is used only in this way.

There exist now only these two expressions belonging to this class. Whereas the older periods had *considered, supposed, seen* (based on F. *considéré, supposé, vu*), English has retained the corresponding active forms, *considering, supposing, seeing (that)*. On the other hand, we still have the pairs: *excepting, except; providing, provided; granting, granted.*

Part 2

Meanings of forms

Meanings of the cases

101 1 The word **case** means primarily a form or modification of a declinable word used to express a certain meaning or to denote a certain relation to another word or words in a clause or sentence. In this restricted sense, two cases only can be distinguished in present English; the one is marked by no distinctive ending, and is employed to express meanings or to denote relations that belong to the nominative, vocative, accusative, and dative in OE. and other inflected languages; the other is the genitive case, which is marked by the ending *s*, e.g. man'*s*, men'*s*, but in plurals formed with an *s* is merely indicated by an apostrophe, e.g. *ladies'* (the pronunciation of which, however, does not differ from that of *lady's* and *ladies*). To this general statement the personal pronouns form an exception, but even in them there remains no distinction in form between accusative and dative, *me, thee, you, us, him, them* performing the functions proper to both these cases, while *her* is used as accusative, genitive, and dative.

Although but few inflexional traces of the old case system have survived to the present day, a *feeling* for case distinctions where no difference of form exists is still evident. An example is seen in those co-ordinate relative clauses in which repetition of the relative pronoun, whether or not in the same form, is felt to be needed when it has different functions in the two clauses, e.g. 'This is a question *which* [subject] has been for ages under discussion, and *that* [object] many philosophers have attempted to solve.' So also when an accusative relative is left unexpressed in the first of two co-ordinate clauses and the relative in the nominative must be expressed in the second clause; e.g. 'He spoke of all the people he had known and *that* (or *who*) were dear to him'; such a form as the following is not normal: 'Behind the unspoken background of things on *which* they agree and need not talk about' [say rather: 'and *that* they need not talk about']. Another example of the influence of such a feeling is the condition that, apart from considerations of rhythm, the accusative and the dative may not be placed indiscriminately when in dependence on the same verb (see §§41.2, 126). But in unstudied speech there is a tendency to get rid of case distinctions and refinements; for example, *me* and *us* are preferred, where possible, to *I* and *we*, and the declension *who, whom* is to a great extent discarded.

OE. had five case-forms, viz. those of the nominative, accusative, genitive, dative, and instrumental, and several declensions, similar to those of German. (A separate form for the vocative is not known in extant OE.) How comes it then that of these numerous forms two only survive in general use?

2 The large majority of OE. masculine and neuter nouns fall under one of two main types of declension: one ('strong'), of which the characteristic endings were -*es* in the genitive, and -*e* in the dative singular, and (except in neuters) -*as* in the nominative and accusative plural; the other ('weak'), of which the characteristic endings were -*an* except in the genitive and dative plural (all dative plurals ending in -*um*). Both of these types continued in modified and simplified form into the ME. period, but it was the 'strong' that was destined to become the prevalent type, and from which our modern case system is derived. Of the second type, there are a few survivals in nouns which take a plural in -*en*, as *oxen* (= OE. *oxan*), *brethren*, and dialectal forms like *housen* (= houses) and *shoon* (= shoes).

The OE. 'strong' declension and its modern representative are here placed side by side for comparison:

	sing.	plur.			sing.	plur.
nom.	} smith	smithas	*nom.*	} smith	smiths
acc.			*acc.*		
gen.	smithes	smitha	*dat.*		
dat.	smithe	smithum	*gen.*	smith's	smiths'

The disturbing influences, firstly, of the Scandinavian invasions and settlements (covering a period of nearly three centuries, from 787 to 1042), and secondly, of the Norman invasion and the consequent influx of French speakers into England (from 1066 onwards) gave rise to extensive changes in the grammatical forms of the language. Such changes are apparent in the language of Northumbria already in the tenth century. In all of these we see at work the efforts of the foreigner, Scandinavian or Norman, to simplify for his own convenience the forms of a language unfamiliar to his ear and tongue, and of the native to meet the foreigner half-way, and adapt his own language to new needs by sacrificing its wealth of form.

3 Thus case and verbal endings came to be modified and simplified, several different inflexions being 'levelled' under a common form, until ultimately, in some instances, the inflexion was entirely lost. All this change was helped on by confusion of forms belonging to different types in the same class of words, both in declensions and in conjugations.

The changes which concern us here are as follows: the vowels *a*, *o*, and *u* in the final syllable became 'levelled' under the form *e*; thus *-as*, *-an* became *-es*, *-en*; *-en* was further reduced in some forms by the loss of the *n*; in very many instances the remaining *e* disappeared also. The genitive singular and nominative plural *-es* finally ceased to be a separate syllable, and sank to *'s*, *s*, except after the consonants *s*, *sh*.

If we apply these facts to the declension of OE. *smith*, it is evident how in the singular two case-forms only survived, while in the plural nominative and accusative became in ME. *smithes*, whence *smiths*, genitive *smithe*, later *smithen* by association with the *-an* declension, dative *smithen*. A further development took place as a result of the ousting of the ending *-en* by the *-es* of the other cases. (The use of an apostrophe to distinguish the genitive in writing appears for the first time towards the end of the sixteenth century.)

4 No account has been taken here of the instrumental case of OE., because it became very early merged in the dative, with which it coincided in form, except in a few words. A survival of this case is found, however, in the construction typified by '*the* more *the* merrier', where *the* represents OE. *thȳ*, *thē*, the instrumental of the demonstrative *thæt* = that.

5 Now, when it is thus shown how three of the singular case-forms have been reduced to one, we must expect to find it difficult, in instances where the case is clearly not the nominative, to say what it really is. For example, in treating the object we have to fall back upon the analogy of OE. and other inflected languages. We say that the single object is in the accusative, because that is the prevalent case for objects in such languages; and where a verb has two objects we may as a rule regard the 'direct' object as an accusative, and the 'indirect' as a dative. We have, therefore, to consider the *relation* expressed by a noun rather than its *form*, that is, we have to consider whether it is subject, object, and so forth.

This question, moreover, is closely connected with that of the order of words in a sentence. If we wish to say 'The cat killed

the bird', we may express the fact by this order of words and
this only. We may not say 'The cat the bird killed', nor use any
other of the four orders in which the elements of this sentence
can be arranged; in fact 'The bird killed the cat' means the
reverse of what is intended, and 'The bird the cat killed' is the
common way of saying 'The bird that the cat killed'. In an
inflected language like Latin, however, we may arrange the three
words 'Felis avem interfecit' in any order we please, because the
form of *felis* and *avem* shows that the first is the subject and
the second the object of *interfecit*. But even in the most highly
inflected languages the order of words plays a considerable part;
where inflexions are extremely few, word-order evidently becomes all important. It is largely in consequence of the loss of
inflexion in English—as well as of the desire, inherent in the
normal progress of thought, to begin with the subject—that the
order of a sentence containing a predicate of the second or third
form is normally

   subject + verb + predicative noun (adjective) *or* object.
Shakespeare's 'Thy name well fits thy faith; thy faith thy name'
would be impossible if the order subject-verb-object were not
fixed.

6 To sum up:—

(i) We have two case-forms in ModE. nouns, the one without
any distinctive ending, and representing historically three cases,
the other having the inflexion *s*, and representing the genitive.

(ii) To speak of a noun as being in the nominative, accusative,
or dative case, is equivalent to saying that the noun would have
been in that case in the corresponding OE. construction, or that
the meaning expressed is such as we associate with that case in
highly inflected languages.

7 The loss of case-inflexion had three important and far-
reaching effects on the structure of the language.

(i) It changed the character of certain constructions. For instance, the range of the nominative was greatly increased as a
result of bringing into prominence the *logical* subject by placing
it at the head of the sentence in the nominative case instead of
in a less conspicuous position in the accusative or dative case.
See §102.

(ii) It contributed to the settling of word-order.

It has just been shown how the loss of an accusative inflexion
made the order subject + verb + object/predicate generally a
necessity.

(iii) It greatly increased the scope and importance of the preposition, just as the decay of verb-inflexions enlarged the scope of the auxiliary verb.

Examples of the substitution of prepositions for the old case-endings will be found in §§105–31. See also §39.

102   The nominative

The nominative is the case of the subject of a finite verb (§29), of a predicative noun in a predicate of the second form (§§6, 35), and of the subject of an absolute clause (§98).

It has been mentioned in §101.7 that, in consequence of the decay of inflexions, a nominative construction has frequently supplanted an oblique case construction. Particular examples of these will now be treated; the instances here are concerned with the bringing into prominence of the thought-subject or logical subject by the substitution of the nominative for the dative.

1 The most conspicuous instance of this is found in the change of impersonal constructions into personal. In OE. verbs taking a dative formed the passive in the same way as similar words do in Latin. Thus like *regi respondetur* (the king is answered, lit. 'it is answered to the king'), we have in OE. (*hit*) *is answerod þæm cyninge* (dative). The latter became in ME. (*it*) *is answered the kinge* (later *king*); the loss of the distinctive dative inflexion *e* easily paved the way for *the king is answered*. The original dative being 'levelled' with the nominative was apprehended as a nominative, and the construction was further extended to pronouns, so that we get *I am* or *he is answered*. (Any such form as this would have been as impossible in OE. as **respondeor* in Latin, or **je suis répondu* in French.) Precisely the same thing has happened with the class of originally impersonal verbs containing *like, long, shame, rue*. In OE. we have (*hit*) *lícath þæm cyninge þæt tō dōnne* = 'it is pleasing to the king to do that'; in ME. this became (*it*) *liketh* or *likes the kinge* (or *king*); whence *the king likes*, and consequently *I like*. With these verbs we have to notice a shift of meaning as well as a change of construction; thus *like*, which originally meant 'to be pleasing', now means 'to be pleased'. Cf. *if you please*, §171.2.

2 *I am woe for't. Woe are we*. These expressions are found in Shakespeare and came down from ME. times. Here we have not only a shifting of case but also of the part of speech: *woe* has become an adjective = sorrowful. This is the result of a process exactly similar to that described above; e.g. OE. *Þæm cyninge is wā* (= To the king is woe) would give ME. *The kinge is wo*, subsequently *the king is woe*, whence *he is woe, we are woe*, &c. The original construction is perpetuated in archaic forms like *Woe is me!* (OE. *wā is mē*) and *Woe worth the day!* where *worth* = OE. *weorthe* 'let (it) become, be', and *the day* is to be parsed as a dative. Chaucer blends the old and the new construction in '*me is* as wo For him as ever *I was* for any man'.

103   The vocative

The vocative (e.g. Speak up, *sir*! Drink, *puppy*, drink! O *wretched countrymen*!) is the case of a noun or a pronoun used interjectionally.

The objective cases

104   The accusative

Its chief uses are:—

> i as the object of transitive verbs (§§8, 37)
> ii as the object of prepositions (§127)
> iii as an adverbial adjunct expressing relations of time, space, measure, or manner (§§105–6)
> iv in exclamations (§57.2).

Historical note on the accusative as the case of the object In OE., as in Latin, Greek, and German, the majority of verbs took an object in the accusative; but there were certain verbs which took it in the genitive and certain others in the dative, the same three cases being also used to express other adverbial relations, as those of time, place, and manner (see §105). A few instances of the genitive and dative as direct object remained in early ME.; but two influences were at work which tended to make these disappear rapidly: (i) the large majority of verbs took the accusative as object, and thus there was a tendency for the accusative to become the universal object-case (just as *-es*, *-s*, weakened from OE. *-as*, has become, except in a few isolated words, the universal plural ending); (ii) the case endings were rapidly becoming 'levelled'; so that (for example) the dative in ME. soon became indistinguishable from the accusative.

The history of the accusative as an adverbial adjunct is similar. Relations of time, space, measure, or manner were expressed in OE. by the accusative, genitive, dative, or (occasionally) instrumental; but by far the majority were in the accusative. By the process of 'levelling' the distinction between accusative and dative became obliterated; moreover, the accusative largely extended its scope by simply supplanting the other cases. The genitive remained in a few idioms which are mentioned in §110.

The use of the accusative in dependence on prepositions presents the same kind of historical development. In OE. all the oblique cases were employed with prepositions, some of which, as in Latin and modern German, took different cases according to the meaning to be expressed. Ultimately, by the 'levelling' process the case after prepositions became the same as the object-case, i.e. the accusative.

In pronouns the form of the object-case is historically that of the *dative*.

105   *Adverbial groups expressing the accusative of time, space, measure, or manner, containing a noun*

The simple adverbial accusative may often be replaced by an equivalent with a preposition, e.g. 'They stayed there some time'

or 'for some time', and the origin of several established phrases
can be shown to be in prepositional groups. Examples:
They went *home another way*.

'Home' represents the OE. *hām*, accusative of *hām*, settlement, dwelling,
and is thus = Latin *domum*. The OE. equivalent of 'another way' would
be in the genitive, *ōthres weges*. We might use an equivalent: 'By another
way'.

He came *full speed*.	Equiv. *at full speed*
Have it *your own way*.	Cf. They did it *in their own way*.
Our friend died *last night*.	Cf. *on the last night* of the Old Year
The windows of the tower face *both ways*.	Cf. *in both directions*
You have been mistaken *all the while*.	Cf. Stay with me *(for) a while*.
They watched and waited *the whole night long*.	Cf. *for the whole night*
I have been nearly *three years* over it.	Cf. I have been at it *for three years*.
You have been *a long time*.	Cf. I have been absent *(for) a long time*.
Bind him *hand and foot*.	
It is the same *all the world* over (see §127.4).	
Months ago he told me that very thing.	
The river is *a mile* broad just here.	Cf. The river is higher *by two feet*.
The sermon lasted *two hours*.	Equiv. *for two hours*
The shot went out to sea *miles* beyond the target.	Cf. The shot travelled *for miles*.
We have been *many voyages*.	Equiv. *on many voyages*
I am *ten years* your senior.	Equiv. I am your senior *by ten years*.
A head taller	Equiv. taller *by a head*
The shares rose *six shillings* today.	Equiv. *by six shillings*

The accusative plays the part of subject in what is called the
accusative and infinitive construction. For full treatment and
examples see §160.

106 A use of quite modern development is what may be called
the **accusative of description,** an adjective-equivalent expressing
such properties of objects as size, colour, age, or price, or the
professions of persons. The accusative may usually be replaced
by *of* with the noun, which was generally the original form of
the expression. Examples:

The plank is not *the right width* (= of the right width).
The towers were exactly *the same height*.
The door was *a dark brown*.
She had hands *the colour of a pickling cabbage*.
What price is that article?
What are potatoes today?
Dukes were *three a penny*.
What age is she? She might be *any age* (or *anything*)
between twenty and thirty.
What trade is he?
What part of speech are these words?

107 The accusative is found in certain exclamatory phrases:
Dear *me*! Goodness *me*! Unhappy *me*! (Cf. L. *me miserum*.)

108 What is sometimes called the *remaining accusative* is
found in the passive form of constructions involving two objects,
where one of the objects becomes the subject of the passive
form, the other remaining unaffected.

active	*passive*
They taught me Latin.	I was taught *Latin* by them.
They allowed him a free hand.	He was allowed *a free hand* by them.
They took care of her.	She was taken *care* of by them.
They paid attention to me.	I was paid *attention* to by them.

109 The accusative is often used to express relations of a very vague kind.
Examples of this are:

(1) its use with normally intransitive verbs followed by a predicative
adjective or adverb; e.g. 'to cry *oneself* hoarse', 'to cry *one's eyes* out',
'to dance *oneself* tired', 'to laugh *a man* down'. These are no doubt
modelled on constructions with transitive verbs like 'to wash one's fore-
head cool', 'to strike a man dead', and so forth. Cf. the use of *it* as a
vague object (see §187.3).

(2) 'They laughed *him* to scorn'. The *him* is originally a dative, but
is now apprehended as an accusative. Compare the similar use in 'he

struck *me* a blow', where *me* seems to be partly dative and partly accusative.

(3) 'To look *things* in the face'; 'to look *a man* through and through'; 'to look *a gift horse* in the mouth'; 'to sleep *the clock* round'. Here the italicized words, if not really objects, are felt to be accusatives. For a discussion of some of these uses, see §127.

110   The genitive

The fundamental meaning of the genitive is 'of', 'in the sphere or scope of'. It is primarily an *adjectival case*, i.e. does the work of an adjective; but as in Latin and Greek, the genitive in OE. acquired adverbial uses from the lost ablative and locative cases. These adverbial meanings have now disappeared as living uses, the inflexion having been superseded largely by the preposition 'of', while many of its uses have been usurped by the accusative. In OE. the case was used in dependence on certain verbs, to denote the object or source of feeling or emotion, what is re- membered or forgotten, what is lacking or supplied, its range being in this respect very much the same as that of the Latin and Greek genitive. It was also used to denote extent of time (*wintres and sumeres*, during winter and summer), point of time (*feorthan gēares*, in the fourth year), space (*fiftēne elna dēop*, fifteen ells deep), and in similar expressions (e.g. *ōthres weges hāmweard*, another way home).

We have seen in §104 how the genitive as a direct object became extinct in early ME., and how its place was supplied.

The history of the expressions of time, place, and extent is exactly similar; they, in course of time, either assumed the 'common case' form, and from their adverbial character may be regarded as being in the accusa- tive in ModE., or else the inflexional meaning was expressed by means of a preposition. In many instances it is possible to use either construction; e.g. we may say 'the fourth year after' or 'in the fourth year after'. Again, often where ME. used the prepositional form, ModE. has the bare accusa- tive, e.g. 'Of fourteene foote it was long' (14th century); here ModE. omits 'of', thus obscuring the fact that the original case was the genitive.

The adverbial genitive survives in a few fossilized words and phrases: *must need*s, *nowaday*s, *go your way*s (cf. German *Gehe deine*s *Weg*es).

111   The only *living* uses of the genitive, therefore, are adject- ival, with the meaning 'belonging to', 'connected with'.

Of these the most common is the **possessive genitive**. As in other languages it may be used:

    (i) attributively: Which is *the doctor's* house?
                 Whose handwriting is this?

(ii) predicatively, i.e. as equivalent to a predicative adjective
(§6):   This house is *the doctor's*; those offices are
                 our lawyer's.
                 Whose is this handwriting?

Note the possible dependence of one possessive on another;
e.g. 'the murderer's horse's tail', 'my father's brother's daughter'.

The possessive genitive may be used with an ellipsis of any
noun, when it is clear from the context what noun is to be
supplied, as

    I have read all Scott's novels, but only a few of *Thackeray's*
    [novels].

But it is especially common with an ellipsis of 'house', 'church',
'shop', or the name of some other building or premises; e.g.
St Paul's = St Paul's church or cathedral; I've just come from
my father's, i.e. my father's house; Go to *the barber's*, *the
butcher's* (understand 'shop'); at *the printer's*.

Such genitives may occur like any noun in any position in
the sentence, as subject, object, &c.: 'I pass *a bookseller's* on
my way home'; 'I will go to *the doctor's*'; '*The doctor's* is on
the other side of the street'.

112   The genitive inflexion may be added not only to a single
word, but to a phrase regarded as a unit. So we may say: '*an
hour or two's* work', '*somebody else's* umbrella', '*a quarter of an
hour's* ride'. This is usually called the 'group genitive'. It is
sometimes carried to extreme, even ludicrous lengths: '*the father
of the child's* remonstrances' (instead of 'the remonstrances of
the child's father'); 'That's *the man I saw yesterday's* son';
'Here's *the passenger that missed the train's* luggage'.

There are some notable variations of the ordinary form of this idiom
in the older language, such as 'I do dine today at the father*'s* of a certain
pupil of mine' (Shakespeare). In ME. occur phrases like 'the emperoure*s*
moder Willelme*s*' (= the Emperor William's mother).

113   The genitive inflexion is often replaced in ModE. by the
preposition 'of'. This occurs even with the ordinary possessive
meaning; thus (in prose) we prefer to say 'the base *of the pillar*',
rather than '*the pillar's* base'; 'the top *of the mountain*', 'the
course *of the month*', not '*the mountain's* top', '*the month's*
course'. In fact the tendency is to use the genitive with names of
persons only. Nevertheless we say '*a hair's* breadth', '*the lion's*
share', 'for *pity's* sake', 'out of *harm's* way', 'a *ship's* car-
penter', 'a *hen's* egg'. No rules can be laid down. English

linguistic feeling alone can be the guide. We say, e.g., 'the sun's rays' or 'the rays of the sun', 'the planet's orbit' or 'the orbit of the planet', 'the flight of (the) ages', but not usually in prose 'the ages' flight', 'the bottom of the page', but not 'the page's bottom'.

The construction with 'of' is preferred as being less ambiguous when the possessor is in the plural. In speech *'the lover's* meeting' is not distinguishable from *'the lovers'* meeting', hence for the sake of distinction it is usual to say 'the meeting *of the lovers'* where the plural genitive is meant.

114 English possesses a peculiar idiom in the use of 'of' with a genitive case immediately following, as in 'This is an old book *of my mother's'*. The construction is most likely to be regarded as elliptical (a plural being understood), e.g. 'This is a book of *my sister's books'*, in which 'of my sister's books' represents the *partitive genitive* of fully inflected languages, so called because it denotes a divided whole, i.e. corresponds to the denominator of a fraction. In ModE. there is no genitive inflexion to be used with this partitive sense; we must use 'of'; e.g. 'many *of the soldiers'*; *'of all men* the most accomplished'; 'he is *of the order* of Knights Templars'; 'all *of us'*; 'what good friends *of mine*!'

OE., and to some extent ME., had a true partitive genitive, used not only with pronouns like *one, some, many,* but also with verbs meaning *to take, receive, give,* and others. But even in OE. we find *of* (with the dative) as an alternative construction; this is in fairly common use in the 1611 Bible. Example: 'He dranc *of the wine'* (Gen. ix 21), where an OE. version has 'he dranc *of thǣm wīne'* (instead of 'he dranc *thǣs wīnes'*); 'She took *of the fruit* thereof' (ibid. iii 6). Chaucer (before 1400) has: *'Of smale houndes* hadde she that she fedde With rosted flessh'.

115 'Of' is now used very extensively where the original genitive denoted what might have been the object of a verb—the **objective genitive**—as in 'their fear *of the enemy* was great' (i.e. they feared the enemy greatly); 'the love *of money'*; 'the slaughter *of thousands'*. The objective meaning is also expressed by other prepositions; e.g. 'love *for* a father', 'search *after* truth'. But this genitive still survives, especially with agent-nouns, as *'my father's* betrayer', *'Fanny's* admirer'. Such an instance as the following is poetical: 'to *sin's* rebuke and *my Creator's* praise' (Shakespeare).

116 Contrast with these *'the enemy's* fear' = 'the fear felt by the enemy', *'a father's* love' = 'the love felt by a father'. The latter is called for distinction the **subjective genitive,** as denoting that to which a thing belongs.

117 The simple **genitive of description** of OE. corresponding to that of Latin, as in *vir magnae probitatis* (= 'a man of great honesty', 'a very honest man'), did not survive, but was replaced by the genitive-equivalent with 'of': 'a writer *of splendid wit'*, 'men *of valour'*, 'a thing *of beauty'*, '*a* debt *of honour'*, 'an attack *of vertigo'*. This is also used to express the material of which a thing consists or is composed, and also the individuals forming a collective unity: 'a ring *of gold'*; 'a frame *of adamant,* a soul *of fire'* (Johnson); 'a field *of buttercups'*, 'the order *of Knights Templars'*, 'a row *of cabbages'*; 'this man *of clay'* (Milton). It is also used predicatively; e.g. 'The flowers are *of a beautiful colour'*; 'Can I be *of any service* to you?'

The genitive, however, with a defining word (often a numeral adjective) may be used to describe, especially in expressions of time and space: '*a moment's* hesitation'; 'a *summer's* day'; '*three weeks'* wages'; '*six months'* work'; 'within *a stone's* throw'; 'the *Thirty Years'* War'; '*a year's* salary' (compare 'the salary *for a year'*); '*twenty-four hours'* notice'; '*an evening's* entertainment'; 'a good *night's* sleep'. So also 'a *dog's* life', '*child's* play', 'a *boys'* book', 'a *doctor's* degree', 'a *busman's* holiday'. But the genitive-equivalent is a not uncommon alternative: 'the work *of a moment'*. In certain groups the inflexional genitive cannot be used; thus we must say 'a boy *of ten years'* (*not* 'a ten years' boy'), 'a man *of thirty'*.

In many instances where Latin uses a genitive of description we should generally use a compound adjective or an adjective-equivalent: *puer oculorum caeruleorum* (lit. 'a boy of blue eyes'), 'a *blue-eyed* boy', 'a boy *with blue eyes'*.

118 The use of the **appositive genitive,** that is, a genitive playing the part of a noun in apposition, was formerly somewhat frequent: 'the government of *Britain's* isle' (Shakespeare); '*Tempe's* classic vale'. The equivalent with 'of' is now usual: 'the city *of Rome'* (= Latin *urbs Roma*); 'the State *of Florida'*; 'the continent *of Africa'*.

But expressions of this kind are limited in range. Though the equivalent with 'of' may be used with names of towns, regions, districts, provinces, and universities, it cannot be used with those of rivers; we cannot now say 'the river *of Thames'*, but must use a noun in apposition, as in Latin. Such differences in language are a matter of usage only and rest on no distinction of meaning. Compare the instances in the following table:

English	*Latin*
the Emperor Augustus (appos.)	Princeps Augustus (appos.)
the word 'pleasure' (appos.)	vox voluptatis (genitive)
the city *of* Rome (gen. equiv.)	urbs Roma (appos.)
the river Nile (appos.)	flumen Nilus (appos.)

119 Akin to the above expressions with 'of' are such as the following, current in colloquial language: 'a brute *of a man*', 'a monster *of a dog*', 'a gem *of a book*', 'the devil *of a job*', and such obsolete expressions as 'He was a ryght good knyght *of a yonge man*' (Malory, *Morte Darthur*, III. xv).

120 The dative
The dative case can no longer be recognized by its form as a distinct case; in nouns, as we have seen in §101.3, the nominative, accusative, and dative have now a common form; in pronouns, the accusative has the same form as the dative, to which it has been assimilated. It is convenient, however, to keep the term for the purpose of preserving syntactical distinctions—as, for example, between the direct and indirect objects—and for comparison with other languages in which it has a distinct case-form.

121 The dative case has two fundamental meanings, conveyed by the prepositions **to** and **for**, which may often be used as dative-equivalents. In OE. the dative had much the same scope of usage as it had in Latin. Some of the processes by which its once extensive use has been restricted have been illustrated in §102.

It must not be assumed that, where either the dative or its equivalent with *to* or *for* is permissible, in the first instance the preposition is omitted. The two constructions are formally distinct.

122 The following are the surviving uses:
 I Meaning 'to'
 A As indirect object (§41) with verbs of giving, providing, offering, leaving, bequeathing, &c.:

He left *his daughter* a large fortune.
I saw Mark Antony offer *him* a crown.—SHAKESPEARE
[A few lines below: Then he offered it *to him* again.]

123 B In dependence on certain adjectives and adverbs: *like, unlike, near (nearest, next), opposite*:

Like *me*, you do not give enough time to reading.
How unlike *him*!
Tell me *what* he is like.
We lived quite near *them*.
The man was in the chair opposite *you*.

124   II Meaning 'for'
The **dative of interest**
(1) With transitive verbs:
Will you write *me* a statement to that effect?
He played *us* a Beethoven sonata.
Make *him* up a parcel of books.
He wants you to cash *him* that cheque.

They found no fault with my Worcestershire perry, which I sold
them for champagne. They drank *me* two bottles.—FIELDING
Villain, I say, knock *me* at this gate,
And rap *me* well, or I'll knock your knave's pate.—SHAKESPEARE

(2) With intransitive verbs:
Your old umbrella stood *me* in good stead.
It will last *the owner* a lifetime.

In old authors, and occasionally (by imitation) in modern authors, we
find *me* or the indefinite *you* inserted in a narrative as a mere expletive
of little meaning. This is usually called the **ethic dative**.
He plucked *me* ope his doublet and offered them his throat to cut.
                          SHAKESPEARE, *Julius Caesar*, I ii 270
A terrible demon of a woman . . . claps *you* an iron cap on her head,
and takes the field when need is.—CARLYLE

125   III The **reflexive dative** (only with pronouns and now archaic), which is used with certain *intransitive* verbs:

She went and sat *her* down over against him.—*Bible*
Stand *thee* close then. I followed *me* close.—SHAKESPEARE
Then lies *him* down the lubber fiend.—MILTON

This is to be distinguished from the reflexive pronoun in the accusative with *transitive* verbs (e.g. I will *lay me* down).

126 *The position of two objects (§§41–3) governed by the same verb*

1 The indirect, whether a noun or a pronoun, precedes the direct when this is a noun:

> She has bought *the boy* a birthday present.
> This saved *my father* much trouble.
> I promised *him* every indulgence.
> Her father left *her* a very pretty fortune.
> Stay and keep *me* company.
> Paint *me* a picture.

2 When both indirect and direct are pronouns, their position is determined by their weight, the lighter of the two usually coming first:

> Tell *him* this.
> Do not send *me* those.
> We will show it *you*.
> I will bring it *him*.

Where the pronouns are of approximately equal weight, there is scope for variety in their position. Thus, 'I cannot lend them *you* now' and 'I cannot lend *you* them now' are equally possible.

3 When the indirect is denoted by *to* or *for*, the direct object usually comes first:

> He taught grammar *to his sons*.
> They meant no good *to us*.
> Bring the book *to me*.
> Will you paint a picture *for us*?

Prepositions

127 1 Prepositions are used with nouns and noun-equivalents to form adjective- and adverb-equivalents. The origins and formations of prepositions are various; many of them are composed of two simple prepositions or adverbs joined together, as *into, out of, within, without,* or are originally phrases, as *beside* = by (the) side (of), *aboard* = on board (of); some have the form of present participles, as *concerning, notwithstanding, touching, following* (for their origin see §100.3), or of past participles, as *except, past*; others were originally adjectives, as *next, round, save*. But the oldest and most commonly used are the simple ones: *after, at, by, for, from, in, of, on, over, till, to, up, with*.

2 The place of prepositions is usually immediately before the word or words to which they belong, as '*in* the house', '*with* rapidity'; but as an archaism and in poetic usage some of them may be placed immediately after the words which they govern:

For having but thought *my heart within*
A treble penance must be done.—SCOTT
As the boat-head wound along
The willowy hills and fields among.—TENNYSON

This was formerly common in poetry, chiefly with prepositions of more than one syllable. (The same order is often found in Latin and Greek.)

While the cock . . .
Stoutly struts *his dames before.*—MILTON
As he were wode [= as if he were mad] he lokyd *hym aboute.*

LYDGATE

That never was ther no word *hem* [= *them*] *bitwene*
Of jelousye.—CHAUCER

The post-position of *notwithstanding* has been dealt with in §100.3 (ii).

3 Now, this fact helps us to discover the *origin* of prepositions. Why should it be possible nowadays, and formerly common, for prepositions to *follow* the words to which they belong? The answer is, that many prepositions have been developed out of adverbs. It will be seen that most of the simple ones enumerated above are still used as adverbs also—all of them, indeed, except *till* and *with*; for *fro* in *to and fro* is cognate with *from*, and *off* is merely a differentiated spelling of *of*. As adverbs, then, these words were originally connected with a verb and not with a noun; they often, however, accompanied a noun standing in an oblique case showing sufficiently clearly its relation to the verb without the addition of the adverb, which was in the first instance superfluous. Thus we should have something like 'He is the town in', 'the town' being in a case which indicated 'rest at a place', the adverb *in* making the meaning more precise. But, in course of time, the adverb lost its close connexion with the verb and became linked to the noun, ultimately taking its position before it and governing it in a certain case.

4 It is obvious that the same adverb could be used with different cases, to indicate different conditions of time, place, and manner; hence it is that we find in OE. (as in Latin, Greek, and German) certain prepositions capable of taking different cases to express different meanings.

How indistinct the line of demarcation between preposition and adverb is may be seen from a consideration of expressions like 'all the world *over*', 'all the year *round*', 'all the way *through*', 'to sleep the clock *round*'. These are apprehended as consisting of an adverbial accusative followed by an adverb, but they seem to have resulted from an inversion of the word-order and a consequent conversion of a preposition into an adverb (e.g. 'all the world over' instead of 'over all the world').

128 By the 'levelling' of the oblique cases which took place in ME., certain shades of meaning conveyed by the use of prepositions with particular cases were lost, but on the other hand the role of the preposition was much extended, as we have seen in §101; the result being that what seems to have been originally a more or less superfluous addition to an adverbial phrase (§127.3) has become a necessary connecting link between nouns and nouns, or verbs and nouns.

The commonest prepositions which have taken the place of the lost or restricted case-endings are: *of*, *from* (= genitive), *to*, *for* (= dative), *at*, *in*, *with*, *by* (= accusative and instrumental). See §§105–26 for various examples.

We have seen in connexion with the partitive genitive (§114) how the substitution of prepositions for case-endings began in OE., where we sometimes find two alternative expressions in use side by side, the one in which the meaning is denoted simply by a case-ending, the other in which it is denoted by a preposition governing its own particular case.

The meanings and uses of the several prepositions must be sought in a dictionary. They do not properly belong to grammar, and are treated in this book only in so far as they may be held to represent lost cases, or are used in special constructions.

129 **By** is the preposition now commonly used to express the agent, e.g. 'He was attended *by* a nurse'. **Of** was formerly much more usual in this sense: 'He was seen *of* Cephas, then *of* the twelve: after that, he was seen *of* above five hundred brethren at once' (*Bible*, 1611).

With often denotes the instrument, means, or accompanying circumstance; e.g. 'He was slain *with* the sword *by* his best friend'; 'My illness was attended *with* fever'. But **by** is very common in certain connexions, e.g. 'The position was gained *by* stealth'.

130 The omission of **of** in certain instances has produced some remarkable expressions. Thus 'a dozen apples' is for 'a dozen *of* apples', *dozen* being a noun (French *douzaine*) and therefore requiring a genitive or genitive-equivalent; similarly 'half a dozen apples' is for 'the half *of* a dozen *of* apples'. The now archaic 'worthy me' is for 'worthy *of* me' ('of me' representing the true genitive of OE. *weorthig min*).

Again, some phrases like (*on*) *this side* have come to be used as prepositions and govern an accusative; e.g. '(on) this side the channel' = '(on) this side *of* the channel'.

131 Prepositions may govern not only nouns and pronouns but also any noun-equivalent: *till late in the night, until now, from above, from here to there, for this once, for ever, for good, from everywhere, all round there, before then,* and the like.

As the result of ellipsis, two prepositions frequently come together: *from under* the table (= something like 'from a place under the table'); *from amongst* the crowd; *to within* an inch; not *till after* the examination; *from beneath* the wings; *up to* the age of seventy; *from over* the way; the fleet consisting *of from* seventeen to twenty sail of the line. In all these cases the ellipsis involves some noun expressing place, time, or measure; but with the prepositional phrase *instead of* we have other kinds of ellipsis: e.g. 'He put it into his pocket *instead of into the drawer*', i.e. 'instead of putting it into the drawer'; 'Things would be worse *instead of better*', i.e. 'instead of being better'.

132 Certain prepositions are capable of governing noun clauses introduced by *that,* thus forming conjunctional phrases, e.g. *in that, except that, save that, notwithstanding that* (= in respect of the fact that, except for the fact that, &c.). These have been modelled upon the much earlier (but now archaic) *after that, before that, till that, for that.*

133 Prepositions are frequently detached from the words they govern and placed at the end of the clause; this occurs chiefly in interrogative and relative sentences or clauses. It is frequent in Old Norse and the modern Scandinavian languages, and may owe its existence in English to Old Norse influence. Examples:

> *Who* are you looking *for*? (instead of: *For whom* are you looking?)
> I have found the book (that) I was looking *for* (= *for which* I was looking).
> This was *what* I was looking *for*. (If the preposition is to take its position before the object, the *what* must be analysed thus: This was *that for which* I was looking.)
> That would be too much to hope *for.*
> Make it clear *who* is referred *to.*
> Some people believe that a preposition is not a suitable word to end a sentence *with* (= *with which* to end a sentence).

But it is also possible in other instances, e.g. where the noun governed by the preposition is separated from it for the sake of emphasis, as in the following:

The binding of the books it is impossible to speak too highly *of.*
The following is an extreme instance (with relative omitted):
The Michaels and Raphaels you hum and buzz
Round the works *of*—BROWNING
There is sometimes superfluous repetition of the preposition, as in:
the weak estate [= condition] *in* which Queen Mary left the realm
in—MILTON

134 Prepositions are attached to the non-finite parts of verbs,
without anything to govern and looking very much like adverbs.
This occurs mainly with verbs constructed with fixed prepositions (§38), as 'a thing to be *thought about*', 'nothing worth
speaking of'. It may, however, occur with any verb and any
preposition, e.g. 'a house not fit to *live in*' (= a house not fit
for habitation). The construction is capable of extension in other
ways: we may say 'unthought-*of*', 'unlooked-*for*', 'undreamt-*of*',
'to be made fun *of*', 'to be set store *by*'; one may hear 'liveable-
in', 'talkable-*to*', 'uncome*at*able', and so on.

This use with an infinitive can be traced back to ME. Thus in the late
Anglo-Saxon Chronicle we have 'me lihtede candles *to æten bi*' = People
lighted candles to eat by, i.e. by which to eat.
The following is an interesting and remarkable illustration of the way
in which such constructions may be extended: 'Mr. St. John . . . was a
lawyer of Lincoln's Inn, known to be of parts and industry, but *untaken
notice of* for practice in Westminster Hall' (Clarendon, *History of the
Rebellion* (1647)).

135 But is a preposition meaning 'except', and like other
prepositions governs the accusative:
No one would have thought of it *but him.*
If, however, a sentence like this is arranged otherwise, the
nominative is very commonly put instead of the accusative:
No one *but he* would have thought of it.
The accusative, in fact, is felt to be inelegant. *But* thus becomes
a conjunction, and the sentence must be regarded as equivalent
to 'No one would have thought of it, *but* he would have thought
of it'.

136 Than, when introducing a contracted comparative clause
(§95.3), has (at least from early ModE. times) been treated as
a preposition and been followed by the accusative. With relative
pronouns the accusative is obligatory (*than whom*, not *than
who*), and its very common use with other pronouns bears
witness to the prepositional character of *than*:
How much older is he *than me?*

It is only by mentally constructing the comparative clause of which 'than me' is the equivalent (cf. §95.3) that one can say 'How much older is he than I?' And this is sometimes considered rather pedantic.

The voices

137 The **active voice** is often used intransitively in English where other languages have a reflexive or passive form:

Corn *sells* at a good price. (= French reflexive *se vend*, German true passive *wird verkauft*)

The weather *keeps* fine.

The chickens will *hatch* out in a fortnight.

The heroes *are girding* for the fight. (= Latin reflexive *se accingunt*)

These oranges *peel* very easily.

Which apples *bake* best?

In the first four examples the intransitive has simply the same meaning as the passive or (in some languages) the reflexive; in the last two it has the quasi-passive sense of 'to admit of being —ed', 'to turn out (well or ill) in the process of —ing'.

138 The forms of the **passive voice** have two distinct meanings:

1 They may express continuous or habitual action, as:

Thousands of letters *are received* daily.

Fruit *was eaten* in large quantities.

When the sense is liable to be ambiguous, this meaning is more unmistakably expressed by the continuous forms: 'are being received', 'was being eaten'.

2 They may express the state resulting from an action, as:

The articles *are sold* (= are in a sold condition, have been sold).

The letter *is* written at last.

For the passive of verbs taking two objects and of verbs constructed with fixed prepositions, see §§42, 39.

Meanings of the moods and tenses

139   Tenses and tense-equivalents

1   Of all the tenses now in use in English, two only are simple, i.e. are expressed by means of a single word—namely, the present and the past (*I write, I wrote*). Around these two the whole

elaborate system of tenses has been built up. In the earliest period of OE., all the various shades of meaning in present, past, and future time could be expressed by these two forms alone. Thus the present tense form was used to express both present and future time; ModE. possesses still a survival or reminiscence of this use (see §140.5). The past tense form had the meanings of the past, past imperfect, present perfect, and (with particles) pluperfect; even now English has no distinctive form (as Greek, Latin, French, &c. have) to express the meaning 'used to', and the past tense is frequently used with pluperfect meaning, as *when they came* for *when they had come* (see §146.1).

2 So long as the language remained simply a means of express-ing thought in speech for everyday purposes, these two tense-forms were adequate, as the various shades of time, present, past, or future, could be indicated by means of adverbs or adverb-equivalents. But when language began to be committed to writing, ambiguities would arise, which, with the increasing complexity of the thoughts to be expressed, made a more elaborate and precise system of tenses necessary. Sentences which might be perfectly understood when spoken might not be in-telligible when written. Therefore we find in later OE. a number of compound tenses coming into use, to express more precisely the meanings of present perfect, pluperfect, and so forth, and towards the close of the OE. period we have the tense system developed almost to its present extent. In some writings, how-ever, the two simple tenses are almost the only ones actually employed.

3 The compound tenses now in use are formed by means of *do* (*did*), *will* (*would*), and *shall* (*should*) with the infinitive, *have* (*had*) with the passive participle, and the verb *to be* with the active participle; i.e. certain short verbs, when used in connexion with certain verb-nouns and verb-adjectives, have lost their independent meaning and have become mere signs of tense. Thus, *he will come* meant originally 'he is willing or resolved to come'; the passing of this into a mere future-equivalent is not difficult to understand if we consider that, when one declares oneself willing or resolved to do something, one has in mind a time which is future, if only by a few moments. Similarly *we shall come* meant 'we have the obligation to come'; the development of this into a simple future-equivalent is equally intelligible. The basic meaning of *I have finished them* is 'I possess them in a finished state, I hold them in a state of com-

pletion'. The original order of the words would naturally be 'I have them finished'. We may still use such a word-order, though it expresses something different from 'I have finished them'; but the subtlety of this difference shows how easily such a form of expression could become a mere present perfect tense. The beginnings of such a process are to be found even in classical Latin, where we have such crystallized phrases as *habeo compertum* = 'I have (it) as a thing ascertained', i.e. 'I have ascertained', the ancestral type anticipating the compound tenses of the Romance languages. With regard to the continuous tenses (e.g. *I am coming*), and the compound forms with the auxiliary *do* (see §§50, 56.3), there has been very slight, if any, weakening of the proper meaning of the auxiliary verb.

The above explanation of the present perfect tense is not applicable to examples like *I have come, he has gone*. The reason is that this is not an 'organic' growth of the language, but is due to the extension of the use of *have*; in the original conjugation we have always 'I *am* come', 'he *is* gone', and *have* has been substituted by assimilation to the present perfect of transitive verbs.

140   Tenses of the indicative

The **present** is used:—

   1 to mark an action as *now going on*, or a state as *now existing*:

> Here he *comes*.
> Whose house *is* that I *see*?
> The war *continues* in all its horror.

An action *now going on* is, however, very frequently expressed by the present continuous (see §145).

   2 to mark an action as *recurring habitually in the present* (habitual present):

> I *write* dozens of letters (every day) (= *am accustomed to write*).
> He *gets* up at six o'clock (every day).
> You *take* water (as a rule), I think.
> Professor B. *lectures* on philosophy (the whole year).

The addition of the 'distributive' phrase ('every day', 'as a rule', &c.) is not always necessary.

The present continuous is also used to express the habitual meaning, but with a difference (see §145).

By an extension of these meanings the present comes to be used:—

   3 to denote what is true at all times (including the present):

Twice two *is* four.

Horses *are* quadrupeds.

Fortune *favours* the brave.

The sacred writer *says*, 'All flesh *is* grass'.

4 in vivid narration of past events, instead of the past (historic present):

News *is* brought of the disaster; the king *does* not dare to appear, but *shuts* himself up in his house.

Such use is especially common in verse.

5 for the future (as in French and German), with point or period of time expressed or implied:

We all *start* in the morning for Paris.

Which of you *go* to London next Saturday?

We *begin* term on Monday.

I shall (will) go as soon as I *am* ready.

The present continuous is also used as a future-equivalent; e.g. I *am going* to town next week; *Are* you *dining* there on Saturday? (not 'Do you dine . . .', which implies habit).

Note the use of the present of 'to hear' in a perfect sense, e.g. 'We *hear* that you have been successful'. 'We hear' == 'We are the recipient of the news', which implies that the action of hearing is really past. 'I learn', 'I gather', 'I am told', 'I am informed' are similarly used. So: 'They tell me that the clock needs attention'.

141 The **past** is used:—

1 to describe an action as *occurring at a moment* or a state as *existing at a moment in the past*:

William the Conqueror *landed* in England in 1066.

Who *took* your hat, *did* you say?

When they *woke*, it *was* broad day.

The war *ended* and there *was* peace at last (i.e. peace came into existence).

This is the usual narrative tense of past time.

A conversational use of this tense is seen in the following, where it expresses that the action or state began a short time— perhaps a few moments only—before the time of speaking, but does not exclude its continuation up to and during the time of speaking:—

A I have been very ill.   *B* I *thought* you *looked* pale.

A I am sorry Mr C. is   *B* Oh, I only *called* to see how
   not in.   he *was*.

N.B.—We have 'looked' and 'was' in accordance with the principle of the sequence of tenses (§153).

So the past continuous; e.g. in the first example we might say: 'I *was thinking* you *were looking* pale'.

2 to describe an action as *going on in the past,* or a state as *then existing* (contemporaneous past):

> The town *was* in an uproar: men *shouted,* women *wept,* dogs *barked.*
> We *argued* for a long time.
> There *was* peace and plenty (i.e. peace and plenty existed).
> As he *hung* in mid air, he *felt* his strength failing.

3 to describe an action as *recurring habitually* or a condition as *constant in the past* (habitual past):

> I *got up* every day at six (= *was accustomed to get up*).
> Scottish kings *were crowned* at Scone (= *used to be crowned*).

142 The **future** is expressed by means of *shall* and *will*, §175, or by the present tense, §140.5.

Future-equivalents in common use are 'to be about to —', 'to be going to —'; they are of almost identical meaning (= 'to be on the point of —ing'), the chief distinction being that the former is literary and the latter colloquial. They may be called 'immediate futures':

> He *is* (*was*) *about to* write = Latin *scripturus est* (*erat*).
> Who *is going to* tell us a story?
> I *was going to* tell you one, but I shall not now.

The colloquial form often conveys the idea of there being something proposed or in prospect:

> They *are going to* make all sorts of new rules in Parliament.

143 The **perfect, pluperfect,** and **future perfect** are used to describe *a present, past, or future state* (*respectively*) *resulting from an existing or continued action regarded as completed at the time of utterance.*

> I *have* now *seen* Paris.
> I *had seen* London before I was ten years old.
> By this time next year I *shall have seen* Berlin.
> I *have heard* it over and over again.
> When I *have been* in the capital, I *have* never *missed* visiting the art galleries.

I wonder when he *will have finished* playing with that garden-roller.

The perfect *I have got* is used colloquially as a present-equivalent = 'I have', 'I possess'. Contrast 'He has got [= has] a bad cold' with 'He has got [= has obtained] no end of prizes in his time'. The other perfect tenses of 'get' bear corresponding meanings.

144   The **secondary future** and **secondary future perfect** describe an action or the completion of an action (respectively) as *in prospect in the past*. In other words, they are the future and future perfect of the past.

I was sure that I *should* soon *return* (= *was about to return*).

I was sure that I *should have returned* by June 10th.

These sentences are the past forms corresponding to—

I am sure that I *shall* soon *return*.

I am sure that I *shall have returned* by June 10th.

Should is here an indicative, and quite distinct from the *should* of conditional sentences, which is a subjunctive.

145   The continuous tenses

All the tenses enumerated above have corresponding continuous forms; these describe an action as *going on* or a state as *existing* in relation to some other action or state expressed or implied and serving as a setting for what is expressed by the *-ing* form.

A period or point of time, present, past, or future, may be either expressed or implied. Thus '*Are* you *enjoying* yourself?' implies 'now' (= at this moment, or during the period of which we are thinking, e.g. during a stay somewhere). When a continuous tense refers to a period, it often implies action taking place in the immediate past or in the near future; e.g. '*I shall be dining* alone all next week'; 'He *had been taking* no exercise for months'.

He *has been writing* the book all over again. [i.e. (say) since he found so many mistakes in it. 'He has written' would mean that the writing of the book is finished; 'he has been writing' does not.]

I believe you *have been travelling* a good deal. [i.e. up to the present, or since you left home, or the like. 'You have travelled a good deal' implies simply experience in the past.]

This time tomorrow we *shall be seeing* him off to France.

I said I *should be coming* back just when he *was thinking*
of going away.

By next January we *shall have been writing* leaders for the
Daily Rag for fifteen years.

Italy and Spain lay hushed beneath the terror of the Inquisi-
tion, while Flanders *was being* purged of heresy by the
stake and the sword.—J. R. GREEN

As we have seen above (§140.5), the continuous present may
also be used with future meaning.

Observe that the simple tenses coincide partly with the continuous tenses, i.e. they may be used to denote the same act or
state. Thus one may say 'I live in Oxford' or 'I am living in
Oxford' indifferently, if one means that Oxford is one's present
place of abode. But to express habit, one generally says 'I live
in Oxford in winter' (i.e. always in winter), *not* 'I am living in
Oxford in winter'. On the other hand, one might say 'I *am
staying* in Oxford for the winter'. Note the difference between
'I don't smoke' and 'I'm not smoking' ('now', 'while I have a
cold').

The continuous forms are sometimes used idiomatically without implying anything 'continuous' or progressive; e.g. 'What
have you *been doing* to that picture?'; 'Someone *has been
tampering* with this lock'. These are different from *have you
done*, *has tampered*; they give an emotional colouring to the
sentence, and express surprise, disgust, impatience, or the like.

146 *The tenses of the indicative in subordinate clauses*

All the tenses of the indicative may occur with their ordinary
meanings in all subordinate clauses where the indicative is
possible. But in the following instances the common usage is
marked by a certain illogicality in the employment of some tenses
instead of others.

1 In subordinate clauses referring to a point of time anterior
to that of the principal clause we have often the past instead of
the pluperfect:

When morning *came* [= *had come*], the fog had cleared
away.

2 In subordinate clauses referring to future time, we commonly have (cf. §81.2b)—

(a) the present instead of the future or future perfect:

The moment he *comes* [= *shall come* or *shall have come*],
I shall go.

If he *comes* [= *shall come*], I shall go.

(*b*) the perfect instead of the future perfect:

As soon as he *has come* [= *shall have come*], I shall go.

The letters must be posted as soon as they *have been stamped* [= *shall have been stamped*].

(*c*) the past or pluperfect instead of the secondary future or future perfect:

As soon as he *came* or *had come* [= *should come* or *should have come*], I was to go.

For the sequence of tenses, see §153.

147   The subjunctive mood

1 The subjunctive is a mood of *will*; in its simplest uses it expresses *desire*, and its chief uses can be traced to this primary meaning, which may be expressed by *shall* or *should*.

The term *subjunctive*, like many other grammatical terms, is misleading and inadequate. It is derived from the Latin *subjunctivus* as used by the Roman grammarians, and means 'proper to be subjoined' (i.e. used in subordinate clauses). It is clear that such a description of the mood is indefensible in two respects: many subordinate clauses do require the subjunctive, but a greater number require the indicative; on the other hand, the subjunctive is required in many simple sentences and main clauses.

2 In modern English the use of the subjunctive mood is much restricted in comparison with its use both in earlier periods of our language and in other languages. Its range in OE. was much the same as in Latin and modern German. In OE. and ME., and even down to Elizabethan times, its use was very free, and we find it in all kinds of subordinate clauses where the verb does not necessarily imply fact. In simple sentences and main clauses of complex sentences there was no restriction put upon its use, whereas now we employ it only in certain kinds of clause and certain stereotyped expressions.

OE. differs from many other languages in having a subjunctive in all dependent statements that do not decidedly express a fact.

3 The subjunctive, therefore, has to a great extent suffered formal decay; and this has been due to two causes, which interacted one upon the other: (1) the levelling of most of the inflexions which distinguished the tenses of the indicative from those of the subjunctive; (2) the loss or decay of precision in expressing thought-distinctions; hence the substitution of indicatives for subjunctives (cf. the loose use of certain tenses of the indicative, §146). The process has been furthered by the

general substitution in subordinate clauses of *may, might, shall* and *should* for the simple subjunctive; e.g. *lest he should die* for *lest he die*. In point of fact, these auxiliary words are themselves in such uses subjunctive in origin, but they have to some extent ceased to be felt as such, while there is nothing in their form to distinguish them from indicatives.

4 It is incorrect to say (as is sometimes said) that the subjunctive, except for *be* and *were*, is an extinct mood. It is true that these are the only distinctively subjunctive forms in common use; but we have seen already in dealing with the cases that, where there has been an extensive decay of inflexions, it is necessary to consider *meaning* rather than *form*; and this principle must be applied here also. A full examination of both the colloquial and the literary language shows that the subjunctive is really a living mood, and that it can never become extinct without the complete disappearance of certain classes of sentences, e.g. the conditional sentences of Class B (§89). In these sentences we have the past referring not to past time but to present or to future time. If we ask 'What is that mood in present English of which the past tense does not necessarily refer to past time?' the answer is 'the subjunctive'. (Cf. §151.)

5 The subjunctive has, however, been *disguised*, except in a few forms, in consequence of the 'levelling' under identical forms of corresponding tenses of the indicative and the subjunctive. To illustrate this, we will take as an example the verb *eat*.

In Old English we have:

Pres. Indic.	Pres. Subj.	Past Indic.	Past Subj.
ic ete	ic ⎫	ic ǣt	ic ⎫
thu itst (etest)	thu ⎬ ete	thu ǣte	thu ⎬ ǣte
he itt (eteth)	he ⎭	he ǣt	he ⎭
we ⎫	we ⎫	we ⎫	we ⎫
ge ⎬ etath	ge ⎬ eten	ge ⎬ ǣton	ge ⎬ ǣten
hi ⎭	hi ⎭	hi ⎭	hi ⎭

In Middle English:

I ete	I ⎫	I eet	I ⎫
thou etest	thou ⎬ ete	thou eete(st	thou ⎬ eete
he eteth, etes	he ⎭	he eet	he ⎭
we ⎫	we ⎫	we ⎫	we ⎫
ye ⎬ eteth,	ye ⎬ ete(n	ye ⎬ eete(n	ye ⎬ eete(n
they ⎭ ete(n	they ⎭	they ⎭	they ⎭

In Modern English:

I eat	I			I ate	I		
thou eatest	thou			thou atest	thou		
he **eats**	he	}	**eat**	he ate	he	}	ate
we ⎫	we			we ⎫	we		
you ⎬ eat	you	}		you ⎬ ate	you	}	
they ⎭	they			they ⎭	they		

From these tables we see that the only surviving difference of form between corresponding tenses of the two moods is in the third person singular of the present (the second person singular may be ignored since it is restricted to poetic and religious use).

6 We are now enabled to establish a test of mood in the many instances in which the form of the verb is no guide: (*a*) in present time, turn the verb in question into the third person singular; e.g. in 'It is necessary that *I remain* here', 'remain' is subjunctive, because we can say 'that *he remain* here' in the same kind of clause; (*b*) in past time, substitute some phrase containing *were*, which would leave us in no doubt about the mood; thus, for 'I wish *I had* a violin', we may substitute 'I wish *it were* possible for me to have a violin'. *Had* here exemplifies the past tense not referring to the past.

Some writers avoid the casual colloquial use of indicative for subjunctive (e.g. 'I wish it *was* possible' instead of '*were* possible').

148   The uses of the subjunctive are as follows:
I—In simple sentences and main clauses
1 To express (i) a wish or request that something may be; (ii) a concession. This is now confined mainly to certain stereotyped, conventional, or traditional phrases (§§54.1, 55). Present tense only.

> God *bless* you!
> Heaven *help* us!
> *May* I live to see it!
> Woe *betide* those who come late.
> So *be* it.   *Be* it so.
> *Be* that as it may, . . . (§55)
> *Suffice* it to say . . .
> Far *be* it from me to . . .

2 To express an unfulfilled wish (§54.2). Now archaic if at all used. Past tense only.

O *could* I feel as I have felt, or be
  what I have been!—BYRON

3 In the main clause of conditional sentences of Class B (§89).
Should, would, could, might, must (§§176.2, 178, 180–82)—and
in archaic use *were* (= would be), *had* (= would have)—are
now the only verbs that occur.

 If I knew, I *would* not tell.

 If thou hadst been here, my brother *had* not died.—*Bible*

An *if*-clause is often suppressed or implied:

 I *should* like to go. [Implying 'If I were allowed' or the like]

 How *would* you express it? [e.g. 'if this is not right'; 'if you
  were asked']

 Anyone *might* see that he is not well. [e.g. 'if they troubled
  to look'].

149 II—In subordinate clauses

Its chief uses are:

1 in conditional sentences of Class B (§89). The tense is either
past (see §§147.4, 151) or pluperfect.

2 in clauses introduced by *if* or *though* subordinated to *as*
or *than* representing a comparative clause (§96):

 I feel as if (as though) I *were* going to fall.

3 in conditional sentences of Class C (§90), where the subjunctive implies *reserve*, or is *restrictive*. 'If it *be* so' = 'granted
that it be so', or almost 'even if it be so'.

4 in noun clauses:

(1) depending on a verb of will, request, or effort, and certain
impersonal expressions (see §§63, 65). This is in regular use in
formal language, statutes, notices, and the like. (The past tense
is not common.)

 It is requested that letters to the editor *be* written on one
  side of the paper only.

 The regulation is that no candidate *take* a book into the
  examination room.

 It is a standing rule in golf-clubs that every one *replace* the
  turf which he cuts up.

(2) depending on the verb 'to wish' and the now archaic
'would' (= I would, §54), to denote that which is wished:

 I wish I *were* (*had* been, *could* have been) there.

 Would he *had* not died!

The origin of the subjunctive in such clauses may be accounted
for by converting them into their original independent form:

(O) were I there! (*expression of wish*, §54): I wish that.

(O) had he not died! I would (= I should wish) that.

The following uses of the subjunctive in subordinate clauses are now confined to the literary language:

5 To mark an action or state as in prospect. This use in temporal clauses is treated in detail in §81. The past subjunctive is not common, and its identity of form with the past indicative often makes the mood doubtful. In a sentence like 'They waited till the ship *sailed*', the mood would be usually indicative; but in 'They intended to wait till the ship *sailed*', it may be regarded either as a subjunctive denoting an action in prospect in the past (= 'till the ship *should* sail'), or as an indicative substituted for subjunctive, just as in 'They intend to wait till the ship *sails*', we have 'sails' where the older language would require 'sail'.

6 In final clauses introduced by *lest* (§84.2):

Lord God of Hosts, be with us yet,

Lest we *forget*, lest we *forget*.—KIPLING

7 In concessive clauses (§93):

Though he *make* every effort, he cannot succeed.

Though he *were* dead, yet shall he live.—*Bible*

8 In general relative clauses (§78):

Calm, but not overcast, he stood

Resigned to the decree, whatever it *were*.—BYRON

However it *be* between nations, certainly it is so between man and man.—BACON

9 In dependent questions (§68):

Whether the Bill *be* as sound as it might be remains for Parliament to discover.

And the headsman with his bare axe ready . . .

Feels if the edge *be* sharp and true.—BYRON

I wonder if Titania *be* awaked.—SHAKESPEARE

All men mused whether he *were* Christ.—*Bible*

'If' is here interrogative = 'whether' (Latin *num*, not *sī*).

150 The following quotations exhibit uses of the subjunctive found in early ModE. writers and continued or revived to some extent in archaic writing of more recent times.

1 Be so true to thyself as thou *be* not false to others.—BACON

[Consecutive clause with prospective meaning: modern equivalent 'as not to be false', §86]

2 *Tide* life, *tide* death, I come without delay.—SHAKESPEARE

[Conditional clause of Class C, §91, with inversion of subject and verb: 'whether life or death (should) happen']

3 Therefore they thought it good you *hear* a play.—SHAKESPEARE

[Noun clause, §63: modern equivalent 'should hear']

4 But other doubt [= fear] possesses me, lest harm
  Befall thee, severed from me.—MILTON
  [Noun clause, §64: modern equivalent 'should befall']
5 Greater love hath no man than this, that a man *lay* down his life
  for his friends.—*Bible*
  [Noun clause with prospective meaning: modern equivalent 'should
  lay']

The survival of the subjunctive in ordinary language in the
United States of America is a noteworthy point of difference
from insular English usage. This American subjunctive, as it may
be called, is typified by such examples as 'The police demanded
that he *move* the car' (insular English 'should move', 'moved');
'The President finds that it is to the advantage of the Western
world that he *do* so' (insular English 'should do'); 'I ask some
thought *be* given that for the moment' (insular English 'should
be'). The usage is gaining ground in England.

We have considered above only those instances in which the
plain subjunctive is used; but in many clauses we may have a
subjunctive-equivalent formed with *shall, should,* or *may*
(*might*), which are themselves originally subjunctives as thus
used; for examples see §§81 foll.; cf. §147.3. Their substitution
for the 'simple' subjunctive dates back to the OE. period.

151 *Tenses of the subjunctive*
The present and past tenses of the subjunctive refer commonly to
present or to future time (see also §§147.4, 149.1):

  Long *live* the Queen!
  Beware lest you *get* entangled in the same snare.
  If you *did* it [i.e. now or in the future], you *would* repent
  it [i.e. in the future].
  If they *could* just see me now!

152 The past subjunctive may, however, refer to past time when
in sequence (see §153) upon a past tense:

  She looked as though she *were* fainting.

153 The **sequence of tenses** is the principle in accordance with
which the tense in a subordinate clause 'follows' or is adjusted
to that of the main clause; thus, in general, when the governing
clause has a present, perfect, or future, the subordinate clause
has a present (*primary sequence*); when the governing clause has
a past or pluperfect, the subordinate clause has a past (*secondary*

sequence). The sequence of tenses applies chiefly to final and noun clauses:

> I *have told* you that you *may* be prepared.
> The master *said* we *might* have a holiday.
> [The master's words were: 'You *may* have a holiday'.]
> He *had* no idea what twice two *was*.
> I *took* care that he *should* not hear me.

Occasionally, however, the tense is not adjusted, e.g. if it is desired to mark something as true universally or at the time of speaking:

> He *had* no idea what economy *means*.
> I *asked* the guard what time the train *starts*.

For other kinds of non-adjustment see §146.

154 The imperative mood

The subject of an imperative (*thou, you*) is not usually expressed (cf. §52); it is found, however, rather frequently in the older language (e.g. 'Go and do *thou* likewise') and is used sometimes colloquially nowadays with a somewhat contemptuous emphasis in prohibitions, e.g. 'Don't *you* go and tell him the secret'.

Non-finite parts of the verb

155 The infinitive

1 The infinitive is in origin and use essentially a neuter abstract noun.

The infinitive has been classed as a mood, in accordance with the usage of Latin grammarians, who called it *modus infinitivus* = 'the indefinite mood'; but its function is not to express the *manner* of an action or to denote the aspect under which it is considered, but to express a doing or a happening without qualification, in the most general terms.

2 In modern English it has one form only, but this is employed in two ways, either (*a*) simply, or (*b*) in dependence on the preposition *to*; e.g.

> I will *write* soon.   I am going *to write*.

3 These two uses represent historically two distinct forms; the simple *write*, for example, is the descendant of OE. *writan*; *to write* is the descendant of OE. *to writenne* (or *writanne*). The first, *writan*, is the nominative and accusative of a noun derived from the verb-stem by the addition of the suffix *–an*, which is equivalent in meaning to the *–ing* of the gerund; the second, *writenne*, *writanne*, is the dative of the same noun, and

was always used with the preposition *tō* ('to') governing it. *Wrītan*, therefore, means 'writing', *tō wrītenne*, 'to or for writing', and sometimes 'in writing'.

4 The way in which these two distinct OE. forms coalesced and became identical was this: *wrītan* became in the ME. period *writen*, then lost the *n*, and settled down in its present form *write*, the final *e* in course of time ceasing to represent any sound: *wrītenne, wrītanne* were levelled under the form *wrītenne*, whence *wrītene, wrīten, write*. (In most verbs the final *e* has entirely disappeared in writing, as *sendan, sende(n), send*.)

To is not found with the uninflected form of the infinitive before the 12th century.

5 In ModE. the infinitive with *to* is much commoner than the bare infinitive. This has come about by the gradual displacement of the latter by the former in many constructions, notably in the use of the infinitive as subject, object, and predicative noun. Thus, the infinitive with *to* lost its datival (i.e. adverbial) meaning, and the preposition became merely the *sign* of an infinitive. Compare 'We made the machine *work*' with 'The machine was made *to work*'; 'Conscience bids you *speak*' with 'Conscience requires you *to speak*'.

From early in the 13th century at least, *for to* was also used as a sign of the infinitive = the simple *to*; this marked a weakening of the use of *for to* = 'in order to', which is of earlier occurrence. These uses are now obsolete in standard speech. See also §157.2.

6 But the *to* is still *not always merely formal*. For example, the infinitive of purpose (e.g. 'I have come *to consult* you') retains its full adverbial meaning and the *to* has its full force of 'with the prospect of', 'for the purpose of'.

7 The infinitive without *to* is used chiefly in dependence on the verbs *shall, will, can, may, must, do, let*, and on simple tenses of *dare* and *need*. So too in dependence on the active voice of the verbs *bid, see, make, hear, feel*; e.g. 'Bid them *come*' (but in the passive 'They were bidden *to come*'); also after *had better, had* or *would rather, sooner* or *rather than*, e.g. 'I would rather *die* than *suffer* so'. See also §40.

156 In accordance with its double origin (§155.3), the uses of the infinitive in present-day English fall into two main groups:

(i) those in which it is a noun-equivalent (§17)
(ii) those in which it is an adverb-equivalent (§19)

Both are exemplified in 'How I like *to be liked* [noun-equivalent], and what I do *to be liked* [adverb-equivalent]' (Lamb).

A As a noun-equivalent, the infinitive may perform all the functions of an ordinary noun, as subject, object, and predicative noun; it always takes *to*, except when governed by a certain class of verbs which are enumerated in §40:

> *To err* (subject) is human, *to forgive* (subject) divine.—POPE
>
> Talking is not always *to converse* (predicative noun).— COWPER
>
> I dare *do* all that may become a man (object).—SHAKESPEARE
>
> Learn *to labour* and *to wait* (objects).
>
> Men fear death as children fear *to go* (object) in the dark.—BACON
>
> Such a world was not a bad place *to live* in (relative clause equivalent).
>
> They love *to see* the flaming forge
>
> And *hear* the bellows roar (objects).

(In the last example *hear* is not properly an instance of the bare infinitive, but is governed by the *to* of *to see*, the force of which is carried on in accordance with idiomatic usage.)

157 Remarks

1 A subject consisting of or containing an infinitive with *to* is regularly anticipated by *it* as a formal subject (§7): *It* is not good *to be happy too soon.*

2 *It is good for us to be here.* In such sentences the infinitive forms only a part of the whole subject-phrase 'for us to be here'. Observe that (i) *for us to be here* is equivalent to a *that*-clause, 'that we should be here'; (ii) the *for us* is felt to be dependent on or at least closely connected with *good*; but (iii) the order may be inverted, '*For us to be here* is good', which shows clearly that the infinitive phrase is now a noun-equivalent and not an adverb-equivalent; (iv) the order *for* + noun or pronoun + infinitive, is invariable. Cf. §63.

The history of this construction appears to be as follows. In OE. we have *gōd is hēr bēon* or *tō bēonne*, i.e. literally 'good is here be' or 'to be'. The infinitive is originally dative (or locative), the sense being 'there is good in being here'. A noun or pronoun in the dative could be added to denote for whom it is good; hence *gōd is ūs hēr tō bēonne* = 'good [it] is for us here to be'. By the substitution of *for us* for *us* (§121) and a slight alteration in order we get the present form 'It is good for us to be here'. Originally the dative depended closely upon the adjective 'good', but in course of time the unity of the group 'good for us' was broken, and it became possible to say 'For us to be here is good'; this no doubt being assisted by the use of 'for to' simply as an equivalent of 'to' with the infinitive. And thus the group introduced by 'for' has become virtually a subject, though the sentence may still be analysed as in OE.

3 The infinitive is not common as one of two objects; with the exception of constructions with the verbs *teach* and *ask*, modern instances are archaic or poetical:

> Teach me *to swim* (= *swimming*: verb-noun).

In many apparently similar cases other explanations are possible. Thus 'Allow me *to pass*' may be taken as equal to 'Allow me *passage*', but many prefer to regard it as an accusative and infinitive construction (§160) = 'Allow *that I pass*'. So with 'Grant me *to know* Thee' = 'Grant me *knowledge* of Thee', or rather 'Grant *that I may know* Thee'.

158 B As an adverb-equivalent, the infinitive with *to* has the meaning of *to* or *for* —*ing*, and sometimes *in respect of* or *in the act of* —*ing*. It is used as follows:

(*a*) To express purpose or destination; this is known as the **infinitive of purpose** (§85) and is found much with verbs denoting motion:

> I called *to see* how you were.
> I pulled up *to have* a rest.
> You have to shout *to be heard*.
> Promises and piecrust are made *to be broken*.—SWIFT

The meaning of purpose may be more fully or unambiguously expressed by *in order to*, and (formerly) by *for to*.

(*b*) With the following verbs the idea of purpose tends to become weakened, though it may never entirely disappear:

> *give, entrust, take, receive,*
> *choose, appoint, send, bring,*
> *help, leave, intend, resolve, purpose* (hence *make up one's mind*),

and others of kindred meaning. So also with equivalent phrases.

> Give me something *to eat*.
> Take this book *to read* on your way.
> An official was appointed *to superintend* the operations.
> I was left *to do* all the work.

After the verb *help*, also, there has been a tendency in recent times to drop the *to*—a usage which is current in American English (e.g. 'Help me *bake* the cakes'), and has no doubt been furthered by the general construction with *hear*, *feel*, &c. (see §155.7).

(c) Depending on certain adjectives (**infinitive of destination**):
fit, able, meet,
bound, ready,
worthy, unworthy,
easy, hard, difficult, possible, impossible,
pleasant, unpleasant,
sure, certain,

and the like. To these must be added the verb-adjectives in *-ed* (passive participles) of the verbs mentioned in (b), as *appointed, destined, inclined,* and the like; also the adjectives *first, last*:

Unfit *to work* Worthy *to be numbered* among heroes
First *to come* and last *to go*
This medicine is pleasant *to take.*
There is not much *to choose* from.
Examples are difficult *to come by.*

Remarks 1 With some of the above adjectives the infinitive has rather an instrumental than a dative meaning, as 'easy *to do*' = 'easy in the doing', Latin *facilis factu*; 'pleasant *to know*'; 'fair *to look upon*'; 'Is my apparel sumptuous *to behold*?' (Shakespeare); 'Deadly *to hear* and deadly *to tell*' (Scott). If this view is taken, there is no need to regard it as elliptical (e.g. 'easy for someone to do'), or as an instance of an active form with passive sense.

2 The adjective-equivalent *about* belongs to this class; e.g. 'about *to fall*'.

(d) Depending on adjectives expressing emotion or desire:
glad, happy, content, relieved, delighted, grieved, sorry, afraid, impatient, anxious, eager, longing,

and the corresponding intransitive verbs:
rejoice, grieve, regret, laugh, weep.

I was extremely glad *to be* thus *freed* for ever from this troublesome fellow.
No one could be happier *to go.*
All wild *to found* a university for maidens—TENNYSON
Three boys in the school had boots—I was mad *to have* them too.—THACKERAY
I regret *to have* to say it.

Remark Most of the above adjectives and verbs may take as an equivalent construction, *of, for,* or *in* with a verb-noun, e.g. 'afraid *of venturing*', 'happy *in being able*', 'to rejoice *at having won* a victory'.

(*e*) After the verb *to be*, or *to have* + object, expressing destination = *for –ing*.

He is not *to go*.

I have something else *to do*.

What have we *to fear?*

The subject is *to be dropped*.

Nothing is *to be done*.

The end was soon *to come*.

That is *to say* . . .

The reason is not far *to seek*.

I was *to have arrived* yesterday.

You have only yourself *to blame*.

On the further development of this infinitive, see §159.

Remark From a modern point of view, this infinitive might be regarded as depending upon a passive participle supplied in thought, as 'He is to go' = 'He is destined to go', 'The end was soon to come' = 'The end was destined soon to come'; but that this is not in all circumstances the origin of the construction is clear from the fact that in OE. we have precisely the existing form.

(*f*) In absolute or independent constructions like the following:

To tell the truth, . . .

To be quite plain with you, . . .

To begin with, . . .

To be brief, . . .

To say nothing of . . .

To sum up, . . .

(*g*) To express result or consequence, especially after a demonstrative adjective, pronoun, or adverb (see §86):

The storm was so fierce as *to tear* up trees by their roots.

I was so weak as *to yield*.

If I live *to finish* the work, I shall be content.

My sister was too young not *to feel* the separation keenly.

The datival character of the infinitive here may be shown by paraphrasing thus: 'I was so weak as (= weak enough) *for yielding*'; 'If I live (i.e. long enough) *for finishing* the work . . .'

(*h*) In dependence on certain intransitive and passive verbs, as *to happen, to seem, to appear, to be seen, heard, felt, supposed, thought, believed, admitted, said, stated, declared, reported, known.* Cf. §24.7.

He happened *to come*.

He was seen *to fall*.

159 **C** To the two chief uses of the infinitive as noun-equivalent and adverb-equivalent (treated under A and B), must be added a third, namely, its employment as an adjective-equivalent. This meaning cannot be regarded as inherent in the infinitival forms, but is to be looked upon rather as a side-development.

The way has been paved for the development of this meaning by the use of the infinitive treated in §158e.

I wasn't the sort of person *to get on* in life.
These shops are *to let*.
It is nothing *to speak of*.
That is easy *to overcome*.
If past experience is anything *to go by* . . .
Obligations are good things *not to be under*.

Here the infinitive is equivalent to the Latin gerundive (e.g. 'which was *to be done*' = L. 'quod erat *faciendum*'), which is a verb-adjective; or to a Latin relative clause (*qui, quae, quod* + subjunctive), which is an adjective-equivalent (§18), e.g. 'There was no general *to send*' = L. 'Nullus erat dux *qui mitteretur*'. Here the infinitive is equivalent to a *predicative* adjective, and this passes easily to an attributive use. Note, however, that even when used attributively, the infinitive must always *follow* the noun it qualifies. Examples (some instances may be explained by ellipsis):

He longed for worlds *to conquer*.
To flee from the wrath *to come*.
The class of people *to be met with* there is not the most select.
[= the class of people that is to be met with]
The sights *to be seen* are not impressive.

The following sentence (from Leigh Hunt), though somewhat exceptional, is instructive as showing the equivalence of the predicative infinitive to an adjective: The good is *to come*, not *past*.

160 **D** The use of the infinitive as the equivalent of a finite verb. *The accusative and infinitive*

1 To a predicate of the third form (verb + object) an infinitive may be added denoting in what respect or by what means the object is affected by the verbal idea, or in what way the latter is limited; e.g. I saw him *fall*. Here the statement that I saw him is amplified by the addition of an adjunct which limits the extent of the statement to saying that the particular action in which I saw

him was that of falling; 'I saw him *in falling, a-falling*'. Similarly
'Command the boy *to appear*' = 'Command the boy *in the
matter of*, or *with respect to appearing*'.

2 Now, in this form of sentence the object of the main verb
and the infinitival adjunct tend to become so closely connected
together in idea as to form an indivisible unit. In this way has
arisen the construction known as the accusative and infinitive, in
which the accusative is regarded as the subject of the infinitive,
so that the whole is equivalent to a subordinate clause with
finite verb.

3 The nature of the connexion between the accusative and the
infinitive (considered as individual members of the group) varies.
Sometimes the two are inseparable because of meaning, e.g. in
'Report declared *him to be dead*'. Here they cannot be separated
syntactically because the verb *declare* cannot be said to take a
personal object; 'him to be dead' is equivalent to a *that*-clause
(viz. 'that he was dead'), which is the usual, though not universal,
equivalent of the accusative and infinitive. On the other hand, in
an instance like 'I heard *the bells ring*' [= 'the ringing of the
bells'], the object of 'heard' and the adjunct 'ring' do not form an
inseparable combination; the sentence is *not* equivalent to 'I
heard *that the bells rang*', which expresses a different notion; the
infinitive retains its full adverbial meaning = *a-ringing, in
ringing*, or *as they rang* (adverb clause).

For an account of the special form of accusative and infinitive
found in 'It is good *for us to be here*', 'The light is too bright *for
me to look at*', 'I shall be glad *for you to help me*', 'There are no
ships *for him to command*' (Pepys), 'This is for you *to do what
you like with*', see §157.2; examples, cf. §63.

161 The infinitive is used as the equivalent of a finite verb with
prospective or deliberative meaning:

1 Without *to*, in certain exclamatory or interrogative sentences with a nominative pronoun as subject (expressed or
implied):

> I *honour* thee? [= Am I to or shall I honour thee?]
> He *tell* me?   She *go*? Not she!
> I, Peter, *perpetrate* so foul a thing!
> I *offer* mischief to so good a king!—'PETER PINDAR'
> Why *carry* the can when there's somebody willing to carry
> it for you?

So, with an indefinite subject unexpressed:

Surrender? Never! Why *be* different?

2 With *to*, in relative clauses and dependent questions having the same subject as the governing clause or an indefinite subject:

I do not know when (where, how, whether) *to go*.

I am at a loss what *to think*.

There was nothing with which *to quench* one's thirst.

162 The split infinitive The construction known—incorrectly —by this name consists in the separation of *to* from the verb stem by means of an adverb, e.g. 'He used *to continually refer* to the subject', instead of 'He used continually to refer', or 'He used to refer continually'. A constant and unguarded use of it is not to be encouraged; some, indeed, would refuse altogether to recognize it, as being inelegant and un-English. (Instances like 'For a time, the Merovings continued *to nominally rule*' are particularly clumsy.) On the other hand, it may be said that its occasional use is of advantage in circumstances where it is desired to avoid ambiguity by indicating in this manner the close connexion of the adverb with the infinitive, and thus preventing its being taken in conjunction with some other word.

163 *The tenses of the infinitive*

The infinitive has two tenses, present and perfect, which have the ordinary meanings belonging to these tenses.

Observe the idiomatic use of the perfect infinitive depending upon *can, may, shall, will* (*could, might, should, would*), *must*, and *ought*. The 'pastness' which belongs strictly to the finite verb is transferred to the infinitive, the reason being that these anomalous verbs (§§172–83) have no past participle; so that instead of saying *he has could do* (= he has been able to do), we must say *he can have done*.

Examples with Latin, French, and German equivalents:

English	Latin	French	German
I could have gone	potui ire or potuissem ire	j'ai pu aller or j'aurais pu aller	ich habe gehen können or ich hätte gehen können
You ought to have spoken	debuisti loqui or debuisses loqui	vous auriez dû parler	Sie hätten sprechen sollen

164 The perfect infinitive which is exemplified in such sentences as 'I should have liked *to have gone*', 'He had intended *to have written*' is much used, but is better avoided. Say rather 'I should have liked *to go*', 'He had intended *to write*'. The 'pastness' belongs to the finite verb and not to the infinitive. Cf. 'He had intended *writing*'.

165   The verb-nouns in –ing, or gerunds
Gerunds are used:—

1 like ordinary nouns, as subject, &c. (cf. §156):
The *digging* of the foundations is very hard labour.
Thank you for *coming*.
What about *walking*?
The following wines are ready for *drinking*.
Now leave *complaining* and begin your tea.

2 with the same construction depending on them as may depend on the verb from which they are formed:
He spoke of there *being a danger* [predicative noun].
Your *being strangers* [predicative noun] is what makes me wish to accompany you.
There are two ways of *meeting the difficulty* [object].
Have you considered *using a fountain pen* [object]?

3 with qualifying adverbial adjuncts:
Staring about aimlessly will do no good.
It's no use *crying over spilt milk*.

4 with qualifying adjectives:
There's *no denying* it.
It's all *your doing*.
There was *much foolish giggling*.

5 as an adjective-equivalent:
I am left with my *starting* problem.
See §18.6.

166   *Constructions of the gerund*
1 Great difficulty was experienced in *procuring money*.
  2 *The procuring of money* was a matter of great difficulty.

These two are now the normal constructions when the gerund has an object, the first construction being the more usual in dependence on a preposition. (In this particular instance the two might be interchanged, but this is not always possible.) In early ModE. (about 1500–1800) three alternatives existed:

procuring money, (*the*) *procuring of money*, and *the procuring money*, this last being very characteristic of the period.

Examples of the obsolete construction:

Shakespeare has: 'in *the delaying death*'; '*the locking up the spirits*'.

> *The mentioning this* makes me add one more particular concerning Archbishop Laud.—BISHOP BURNET (ante 1715).

The following passage from Bacon is interesting as containing two of the alternatives current at the time: 'Concerning the means *of procuring unity*, men must beware that in *the procuring or muniting* [= fortifying] *of religious unity*, they do not dissolve and deface the laws of charity'.

The old construction survives in the traditional formula *The Trooping the Colour*.

Notice the following alternative constructions, the first involving the use of the gerund, the second that of the verb adjective in *–ing* (active participle):

> What is the use of *his coming*?—of *him coming*?
>
> He spoke of *its being* cold—*it being* cold.

Some people insist that the first of these constructions should always be used. But the second involves nothing illogical or inconsistent with other uses of the participle, which may be generally paraphrased by 'in the act of —ing'. We find a good instance in Clarendon of the gerund qualified by a possessive: 'Sunday passed without *any man's taking* notice of *the keeper's being* absent'. So Jane Austen: 'One never thinks of *married men's being* beaux'.

167 The use of the gerund governed by *a* (= *in*), e.g. 'I went with other merchants *a-pearl-fishing*', 'In the days of Noah, while the ark was *a preparing*' (*Bible*), is now archaic and dialectal; but there is a literary survival of it, with the preposition dropped, in 'The church is *building*' (= a-building, in course of building), 'The reformation must still be *doing*, never done', 'The book is *reprinting*'. (Contrast 'Forty and six years was this temple *in building*'—*Bible*.)

On account of the identity of form between the verb-noun and verb-adjective in *–ing*, it is sometimes difficult to determine to which part of speech a particular form belongs. In the following, for example, we may regard *dressing*, &c. either as participles agreeing with the subject, or as gerunds (= *a-dressing*, &c.):

What a long time you are *dressing*!

He was too much occupied *watching* the passers-by to notice what was said.

168 The gerund must be handled carefully with respect to its reference to the rest of the sentence. Do not write, e.g.: 'After *fighting* the flames for several hours the ship was abandoned'. Here, *fighting* refers grammatically to 'the ship', which makes nonsense; say: 'After they (the crew, &c.) had been fighting . . .' or 'After fighting the flames . . . the crew abandoned the ship'. Correct the following: 'By *pouring* hard peas upon the hatches they became so slippery that the boarders could not stand'. [Who poured?]

169   The verb-adjectives or participles

The participles are used:—

1 as predicative adjectives:

The city lies *sleeping*.

I see him *coming*.

The birds came *hopping* about the windows.

We saw the metal *beaten* into a thin plate.

In compound tenses ('He is *writing*', 'He has *written*', 'Many letters are *written* every day') the participle was originally a predicative adjective (cf. §139.3): 'He has *written* a letter' = 'He has a letter *written*'. Both constructions survive, but now with a difference of meaning; cf. French 'Il a *écrit* une lettre' and 'Il a une lettre *écrite*' (= Latin 'Habet epistulam *scriptam*'). So 'I have *finished* my work'; 'I have my work *finished*'.

N.B.—Contrast, from an historical point of view, 'He *is building* a church', and 'The church *is building*' (§167).

The fully adjectival sense of many participles is a lexicographical matter; thus *amusing, comforting, devastating, filling, killing, rewarding, satisfying, yielding*; *amused, contented, devoted, exasperated*.

2 as attributes:

He was a *squeezing, grasping, scraping, clutching*, covetous old sinner.

A room *overlooking* the garden.

Science is *organized* knowledge.—HERBERT SPENCER

In phrasal use the verb-adjective often *follows* the noun: for the time *being*; for the third year *running*; the last day of September next *following*; any man *living*; in times *past*.

3 as noun-equivalents: the *living*; the *wounded*; the *deceased*; the *blessed*.

4 in the 'absolute construction' (nominative absolute, §98, where the full treatment will be found).

NOTE—The form employed in the following example is not now common in prose, except in such established phrases as *this* (*which*) *done*, *this said* (which appear to be imitations of Latin or French, *hoc* (*quo*) *facto*, *cela fait*, &c.), *all things considered*.

> All things thus *prepared*, and so many lords *driven* and *kept* from the house besides the bishops, and they that were staying there *instructed* how to carry themselves, they [the Parliamentarians] resolved once more to try whether the House of Peers would be induced to join in the business of the militia (Clarendon, 1647).

The forms *being prepared*, *having been prepared*, are now preferred. The first of these denotes strictly an action going on or a state existing, the second the completion of an action; but in practice they are as a rule used indiscriminately.

170 The participle should always have a proper 'subject of reference'. In a sentence like the following the word to which the participle refers by its grammatical position is not that with which it is meant to be connected in sense: '*Born* in 1850, a part of his education was received at Eton'. Say rather: '*Born* in 1850, *he* received part of his education at Eton'. Cf. §99. This must be particularly observed in the case of the elliptical 'while fighting', 'though fighting', &c., in which a *conjunction* is freely coupled with a participle. Cf. §168.

Impersonal verbs

171 1 This term is applied to such verbs as are used in the third person singular with or without a vague subject 'it' to express without particular reference to a person that an action is taking place or a state existing. In the OE. and ME. periods they were more numerous than now; those which remain in use are chiefly verbs denoting natural phenomena, especially states of the weather, as *it rains*, *it snows*, *it thunders*, and similar expressions formed with the verb 'to be', as *it is warm*, *it is frosty*, *it is day*, *it is time*. 'It rains' = 'there is rain', 'rain is falling'. So with extensions or modifications of these phrases, e.g. 'It feels like rain'; 'It is clouding over'; 'It is raining cats and dogs'. So also with 'It is so'; 'It doesn't matter'; 'If it were not for . . .'

2 Many verbs originally belonging to this class have lost their impersonal use and have come to be employed solely with personal subjects, by the process described in §102. We no longer say 'it liked him', but 'he liked'; the same has happened with French-derived words such as 'repent' and 'please'. 'It repents me' persisted as an archaism, but 'I repent' is the regular construction. The true impersonal use of 'please', without formal subject of any kind, has survived in 'if you please', where 'you' is historically not the subject of 'please', but a dative case depending on it; the expression thus corresponding exactly to the Latin *si tibi placeat* 'if it please you' (subjunctive). But since 'you' is ambiguous as to its case-form, it was easily taken as nominative, and hence we get unmistakably the fully developed personal construction in 'if I please', 'if they please'.

3 As in Latin and Greek, so often in OE., impersonal verbs which took an oblique case denoting the person affected had no grammatical subject. Thus OE. *mē thyrst* (or *thyrsteth*) '(it) thirsts me', 'I thirst'; *thē lyst* (or *lysteth*) '(it) pleases thee'; so ME. *wel oughte us werche* 'well (it) behoved us to work'.

But in the ME. period the use of 'it', which occurred fairly frequently in OE., became regular both with native and with adopted verbs. The construction without *it* still survives, however, in certain crystallized expressions, as in the antiquated *methinks* (OE. *mē thyncth* 'it seems to me') and *meseems*, and, as we have seen above, in *if you please*. We find it also in the modern language in uses like the following, especially in *as-* and *than*-clauses:

I shall act as *seems* best.
This remarkable general brought about the end of the war much sooner than *was expected*.
As *has been said* already; as *will appear*; as often *happened*; as well as *can be expected*; as far as in me *lies*; as *regards* the question of money; no more than *is* right and just.

The formula 'as *follows*', introducing an enumeration, is likewise an instance of this construction. Through ignorance of its impersonal character, it has sometimes been perverted to 'as follow'.

4 An infinitive with dative or locative meaning is often added to an impersonal verb to limit the manner or respect in which

the action of the verb takes place. Thus we may say simply *it hurts me* = 'there is hurt or pain to me', but we may specify the manner by saying *it hurts me to write* = 'there is hurt to me in writing'. In such instances, the 'it' has come to assume a double function, because it not only indicates the vagueness of the verbal notion, but also serves as a formal subject to anticipate the infinitive, which expresses the logical subject of the sentence: *it hurts me to write* = 'to write hurts me'. This is like *it is easy to write* = 'to write is easy' (§6). There are therefore two possible ways of analysing such a sentence:

(1) To write (*subject*) ⎫
    It (*formal subject*) ⎬ hurts (*verb*)
(2) It (*subject*) hurts (*verb*) to write (*adjunct*).

In a sentence like *It is time to go*, however, the second analysis only is possible, because we cannot convert it into 'To go is time'.

Anomalous verbs

172 I Shall and **will—should** and **would**

Shall has reference to the performance of an action or the existence of a state viewed as lying outside or beyond the power or will of the speaker. *Will* has reference to such an action or state viewed as determined by the speaker's power or desire. The fundamental meaning of *shall* is 'to be under a necessity', 'to be obliged'. It may often be paraphrased by 'am to', 'is to', 'are to'. The fundamental meaning of *will* is 'resolve, intend'. The past tenses *should* and *would* have meanings corresponding to their respective presents. (Where the past tenses follow the meanings of the present tenses, they will be ranged under the latter in the following sections without further comment; the peculiar uses will receive separate treatment.)

The traditional idiomatic use of *shall* and *will* is one of the points that are regarded as infallible tests of the true English speaker; it offers peculiar difficulties to Scots, Irishmen, and Americans, the main difference being that these use *will* in many places where the Englishman uses *shall*.

173 Shall and **will** (present indicatives) and **should** and **would** (past indicatives) are used:

A with independent meaning—*shall* denoting obligation, necessity, or permission; *will* denoting resolve or willingness.

I *will* (= am resolved to) live a bachelor.

Will you (= do you intend or wish to) take it with you, or *shall* I (= am I to) send it?

We *will* (= intend to) send someone to fetch you.

He *will* (= is determined to) go, say what you may.

He *would* (= was determined to) go, say what I might.

I *would* not (= was unwilling, refused to) answer him, when he spoke to me yesterday.

Thou *shalt* not steal.

You (he, they) *shall* go this instant.

Where the tree falls, there it *shall* (= is destined to) lie.

He found the country in a state of unrest, for reasons which you *shall* hear.

You *shall* repay me at your convenience.

It seemed to him that he could nowhere find in his heart the chords that *should* answer directly to that music.

Wilt thou (= art thou resolved to) have this woman to be thy wedded wife?

Answer: I *will*.

Walking along the High Street, whom *should* I (he, we, they) meet (= was I, were we, &c. to meet) but my cousin Tom?

Note the following peculiarities:

1 In the second person *will* is sometimes used to express a request or command; e.g. 'Will you tell me the time, please?'; 'You *will* light my fire at 7 o'clock'; 'You *will* not go out today; you *will* stay in and work'; 'You *will* do nothing of the sort'. So in a public instruction: 'Passengers for X *will* alight at Y'. Note also: 'Will you stop that noise?'; 'I wish you *would* be quiet'.

2 *Shall* is sometimes stronger than *will*; e.g. 'You will not go away?— I *shall*' (i.e. nobody shall stop me).

174 The past subjunctives **should** and **would** are similarly used in the main clauses of conditional sentences of Class B (§89):

Even if I knew, I *would* not tell (= *should* not *be willing* to tell).

Wert thou creation's lord, thou *shouldst* not taunt me thus (= *wouldst* not *be permitted* to taunt me thus).

Contrast their use as auxiliaries of mood in subordinate clauses (§176.2).

The past subjunctive **should** is used in all persons virtually as a present indicative—like *ought*, and with the same meaning:

You *should* not say that (= You *ought* not to say that =

properly 'you *would* be bound not to say that', hence
'it *is* right for you not to say that').

I know that I *should* not do it, but I cannot help it.

We *should* be starting soon.

The weather *should* be fair but cloudy most of the day.

The past indicative **would** has often the sense of 'used to',
denoting past habitual action. (*Will* similarly expresses present
habitual action; e.g. 'Courage *will* come and go' (Sheridan);
'Accidents *will* happen'.)

His mind seemed unhinged; he *would* be always muttering
as he went along.

Would denotes also what might have been expected:

My shoelace *would* break just when I wanted to catch
my 'bus.

175   B as auxiliaries of tense.

A mere future event regarded as independent of the present
will is expressed by **shall** in the first person and **will** in the second
and third. (The pasts *should* and *would* are used in dependence
on verbs of past time.)

I *shall* soon be an old man.

Anyone *will* tell you the way if you ask.

If you stay here, you *will* see him pass.

I knew that if you stayed here you *would* see him pass.

Shall and *will* may be used together to express all possibilities
of future action:

Gather me all you can, and do it quickly, or I *will* and
shall do without it.—JOHNSON

I never *shall* see, and I never *will* see, any good in extrava-
gant idleness.—TROLLOPE

The future is not uncommonly employed to express an in-
ferential fact of present time:

This *will* no doubt be the book he referred to.

I expect you *will* have read about the gala.

In independent questions:—

(*a*) In the first and third persons *shall* and *will* are used as in independent statements:

Shall we see the king in the procession?

Will the parcels be sent out tomorrow?

(*b*) But in the second person that auxiliary is used which is expected in
the answer:

Shall you go to London tomorrow? (The expected answer is 'I
shall'.)

The substitution of *will* would convert the sentence into a kind of request. See above §173. A shift of usage has been going on for some time, with the extension of *will* to places where *shall* was considered appropriate.

176 C as auxiliaries of mood—subjunctives and subjunctive-equivalents.

1 In the main clauses of conditional sentences of Class B, **should** is used in the first person and **would** in the second and third (cf. §175). For examples see §89.

> Though you said it a thousand times, I *should* not believe it—no one *would* believe it.

2 In certain subordinate clauses **shall** or **should** is used in all three persons to form a subjunctive-equivalent: (*a*) in clauses in which the action is marked as contemplated or in prospect, §§78, 81.2b, 82.2, 84, 88; (*b*) in conditional clauses of Class C, §90; (*c*) in certain dependent statements and commands, §§60, 62–3, 65.

Note that *should* is used (i) as the equivalent of a *present* subjunctive; (ii) as the equivalent of a *past* subjunctive in sequence upon a past tense.

(*a*) There will I hide thee, till life *shall* end.
> He remained at Lyons till the point in dispute with the king *should* be decided.
> Permission to use the reading-room will be withdrawn from any person who *shall* write on any part of a printed book.

(*b*) If the king *should* fall,⎫
> *Should* the king fall,⎬ he will fall by fair fighting.

> I am sorry that you *should* be so angry (Latin *quod sis tam iratus*).

(*c*) It is (was) natural that I *should* spend the time with my family.
> My aunt intends that you *shall* accompany us.
> I undertake that you *shall* not be the loser by it.
> I took care that he *should* not detect me.

177 II Can, could—may, might—must
Can expresses *ability*. It has always independent meaning, i.e. it is not used to form tense- or mood-equivalents. 'I can' originally meant 'I know' (cf. §40.1); with an infinitive it came to mean 'I know how', and hence 'I am able to', 'I have power to'.

178 **Could** is either (1) past indicative = *was able*; e.g. 'At a very early age he *could* read and write Latin'; 'He asked me whether I *could* speak Latin' (corresponding independent question, '*Can* you speak Latin?'); or (2) past subjunctive = *should* or *would be able*; e.g. 'If I *could* tell you, you may be sure I would' (§89); 'Where *could* he sleep if he came?'; '*Could* you see him now?'

It is not always possible to tell what mood *could* is, apart from the context. Thus 'How *could* you do it?' might mean either (1) How did you find it in your heart to do it? or (2) How would you be able to do it?

179 May expresses *possibility* or *permissibility*. 'I may' originally meant what 'I can' means now, but when 'can' encroached on the meaning of 'may', the latter began to assume the new meanings which it now bears.

May is used (1) as an indicative and (2) as an auxiliary of mood, forming a subjunctive-equivalent.

(1) As an indicative it has two meanings. Thus, 'I may come', when written,* is ambiguous; it may mean 'It is possible that I shall come' or 'I am permitted to come'; e.g. in 'I may come, but don't wait for me' it denotes possibility, while in 'I may come if I like' it denotes permissibility.

(2) As a subjunctive-equivalent it is used (i) in wishes as to the future (§54.1); (ii) in certain clauses where the action is marked as contemplated or in prospect (see §§60–4, 78–9, 84). Even in these the independent meaning is often traceable:

I fear the dog *may* bite you.
Although it *may* seem absurd, it is true.
May it not be spoken in vain!
God grant that it *may* not be spoken in vain.

180 Might is the past tense of *may*, and partakes of all its uses:
I asked if I *might* come. (Cf. I asked: 'May I come?') [past indicative]
I feared the dog *might* bite you.

Might, like *could*, is sometimes a past subjunctive with independent meaning; thus 'I might come' may mean not only 'It was possible for me to come', 'I was allowed to come' (past indicative); e.g. in 'He said that I *might* come' [if I chose]; but

---

* In speaking, the intonation of 'I may come' would leave no doubt as to its meaning.

also 'It would be possible for me to come', 'I should be allowed to come'. Its use as a past subjunctive is confined to conditional statements, dependent or independent, and the main clauses of conditional sentences:

Anyone *might* do the same [if he had the chance].
Can anyone say he *might* not do the same?
If I *might* suggest, I would say . . .

Hence its use in mild requests: '*Might* I be allowed to suggest . . .?'

181   Must expresses *necessity* and *obligation*. 'He must go' = 'He is bound to go'; 'It is necessary for him to go'. Historically, *must* is the past tense of OE. *mōt* 'I am allowed'. Its use as a present tense originates in its use as a past subjunctive referring to present time. 'He must go' = 'He *would* be bound to go (if . . .)'; there being a natural tendency in speaking of obligation to soften harshness by using the form of a conditional sentence.

182   As a past *subjunctive* in conditional sentences it means 'would be bound':

If he had looked, he *must* have seen the light of the approaching train [= he would have been bound to see].
Contrast: From these few ruins we may gather what the city *must* have been like in its prime [= is bound to have been like].

183   The use of *must* as a past *indicative* is now limited to actual or virtual Oratio Obliqua; i.e. the clause containing *must* is subordinated either formally or *in thought* to a verb in past time:*

The desire for the boots was so great that have them I *must* at any rate. [Reported form of 'I *must* have them']
He said he *must* speak with his master. [Reported form of 'I *must* speak with my master']
He could not be idle: he *must* always be doing something. [His thoughts were: 'I *must* always be doing something']
There he lay in the dungeon. Yet a few hours more, and he *must* die a shameful death. [He thought: 'A few hours more, and I *must* die a shameful death']

---

* If we are to turn 'When he comes, I *must* go' into the past, we must say: 'When he came, I *had* (or *was obliged*) *to* go'; *must* is here impossible.

Adjectives

184   The adjective is used:
   1   as a predicative adjective: see §§6, 17
   2   as an attribute: see §14
   3   as a noun-equivalent: see §17.3.

Attributive adjectives sometimes *follow* the noun, particularly in technical designations: letters *patent*, heir *apparent* (*presumptive*), lords *temporal* and *spiritual*, poet *laureate*, consul *general*, body *politic*, court *martial*, time *immemorial*. So also: Sunday *next* (*last*), a diphthong *proper*, the amount *accruing* (*outstanding*, *owing*), for the time *being*, a guess *pure and simple*.

When used as noun-equivalents, adjectives (i) may be preceded by *the*, e.g. '*The poor* (= those who are poor, poor people) ye have always with you'; or (ii) may stand unqualified, but then there must be two or more adjectives coupled together, e.g. '*big* and *little*', '*old* and *young*', 'through *thick* and *thin*', 'from *grave* to *gay*, from *lively* to *severe*'.

'The *old*' can now mean only (i) 'old men or women' (plural), never 'the old man'. But the latter use was formerly common, e.g. 'And when the devil was cast out, the *dumb* spake' (OE. '*se dumba spræc*'); (ii) 'that which is old'.

For examples see §§17.3, 199.6.

Pronouns, their adjectives and adverbs

185   Personal pronouns
1 Personal pronouns, with the exception of *you* and *it*, have distinct forms for the accusative-dative case, which may help us to determine the case of nouns in similar constructions, where the form of the noun of course gives no clue. This is shown, for instance, with *but* following a comparative, negative, or interrogative word; thus from the analogy of 'None but *they* have a right to rule', we may conclude that in 'None but *the brave* deserves the fair', 'the brave' is in the nominative; and from a sentence such as 'Was anybody there but *him*?' we may infer that in 'Were they all there but *the captain*?', 'the captain' is accusative.

2 Personal pronouns are used, like nouns, as subject, as object, and in the predicative relation (predicative pronoun). For *It is I, It is me*, see §36.4.

3 The use of *thou* and *ye* is confined in present-day English
to the language of religion.

Ye is historically the nominative, and *you* the oblique form; *you* as
a nominative has simply usurped the place of *ye*. In the Authorized version
of the Bible (1611), the distinction is throughout carefully preserved (with
a very few exceptions) between *ye* (which represents the OE. nominative
gē), and *you* (which represents the OE. accusative-dative *ēow*). But long
before this, *you* had begun to displace *ye* as nominative, and *ye* in turn
to be used as an oblique case; Shakespeare has instances, e.g. 'I do beseech
ye, if *you* bear me hard . . .'.

4 *We* is used for *I* as a 'plural of majesty' by sovereigns
and other persons of high rank when using formal or official
language:

> *We* have made inquiry of you, and *we* hear
> Such goodness of your justice, that *our* soul
> Cannot but yield you forth to public thanks.—SHAKESPEARE

(A Duke is speaking; later on in the scene, talking familiarly,
he uses 'I'.)

The origin of this usage may be seen in OE., where the King frequently
in the early part of a document made use of *ic* = 'I', and then went on
with *wē*, meaning 'I and my advisers', 'I and my council'.

We is also used to avoid the repetition of 'I'. One of the
commonest instances of this is what is termed 'the editorial *we*',
which is used by writers of newspaper articles; e.g.

> *We* do not say that everything in these essays is as good
>   as what *we* have quoted.

Somewhat similar is the use of 'us' in the colloquial 'Let's
see'. Cf. French *Voyons*.

We is often employed colloquially, like 'you', as an indefinite
pronoun = 'one': *We* don't usually think of Oxford in these
terms; It's our own fault if *we* miss the chance; *You* never
know; *You* never can tell.

5 The personal pronouns of the third person are sometimes
used to repeat the subject of a sentence. In ordinary speech it
is a vulgarism or a mark of carelessness, or may be due to
hesitation; in literary language, it may give a picturesque or
graphic touch to a sentence. It is not infrequent when the subject
and its verb are far apart, when its insertion may serve to resume
the thread of the discourse. It was a common feature of early
periods of the language.

> The Lord thy God, *he* is God.—*Bible*
> A frog *he* would a-wooing go.
> Year after year my stock *it* grew.—WORDSWORTH
> The prophets, do *they* live for ever?—*Bible*

The repetition may be made by placing the pronoun first, as in:—

> *He* is a handsome fellow, that cousin of yours.
>
> His prayer *he* saith, this patient holy man.—KEATS
>
> *It* was worth remembering, that scene.

Similarly, when the object is detached for emphasis, it may be repeated by a pronoun:

> The lofty city, he layeth *it* low.—*Bible*

Extraposition occurs also in questions; e.g. 'The strike, is *it* over?'

6 *He, she, it* are essentially *demonstrative* pronouns, and mean respectively 'that or the man, woman, or thing'. This comes out clearly in expressions (now archaic) like 'he of the bottomless pit', 'he of the mailed fist', 'she of the auburn hair'.

186 It

The uses of the pronoun *it* may be classified under two headings:

I   Those in which *it* represents some noun or noun-equivalent.

1 Under this heading come the instances in which it has the full meaning properly belonging to a personal pronoun as standing for a noun. As with other personal pronouns, the reference of *it* to the noun it represents is not always made without ambiguity; e.g. 'When the baby has finished the bottle, *it* should be unscrewed and put under the tap'; 'If the baby will not drink cold milk, boil *it*'. Such ludicrous awkwardness may be avoided by a change of phrasing: 'When the bottle is finished . . .'; '. . . use boiled milk'.

2 Secondly, we have its use as a *formal subject* (§7) in which *it* represents an infinitive or gerund or a subordinate clause following:

> *It* is impossible *to deny the existence of evil* = To deny the existence of evil is impossible.
>
> *It* is fully expected *that the result will be favourable* = That the result will be favourable is fully expected.
>
> *It* is dangerous *playing with explosives.*
>
> *It* is no use *talking like that.*

English idiom now frequently requires that a noun clause or an infinitive playing the part of an object should be anticipated by *it*; this gives rise to what may be correspondingly called a *formal object*:

> to find *it* easy to . . .
>
> to think *it* hard (good, right) that . . .

to bring *it* about that . . .

to see to *it* that . . .

The reason for this insertion of *it* seems to be that the noun clause is not clearly felt to be the object of the sentence as it appears to be in Latin or French, where we should have simply:

efficere ut . . . curare ut . . .

faire que . . . trouver bon de . . .

The construction without *it*, however, is idiomatic in a few expressions; e.g. 'He tried to make out that he was the heir' [not 'make it out']; 'If you think fit to take such steps . . .'

3 *It* frequently has the meaning of 'the person or thing thought of, mentioned, under discussion, or in question':

Who is *it*? (= the person who has come, is at the door, &c.)

It is the postman. *It* is the prince and princess.

Well, what is *it*? [that you want, are thinking of, &c.; that is happening, &c.]

Cf. the similar use of *that* in 'Is *that* you?'

187 **II** Those uses in which *it* means something like 'things' or 'things in general'.

1 The greater number of these come under the head of impersonal verbs (§171) and kindred uses:

It is warm today.

So *it* says in the book. (= There is a saying to this effect . . .)

This applies only to the grown up; with children *it* is different (= there is a difference, things are different).

It is not thus with music; still less is *it* so with poetry.

It looks as if we were going to have a storm.

2 Occasionally 'it is' = French *il y a* with expressions of time:

It is some time since I saw you.

In ME. *it is* often = 'there is', as: *It was* once a kynge.

3 As an object with indeterminate meaning after an intransitive verb (cf. §109):

Come and trip *it* as you go

On the light fantastic toe.—MILTON

Foot *it* featly here and there.—SHAKESPEARE

Lord Angelo dukes *it* well.—SHAKESPEARE

Similarly in colloquial and slang expressions like 'to rough *it*', 'to go *it*'.

188   Possessive adjectives and pronouns
The possessive meaning of the adjectives becomes as wide and
vague as it is with nouns, and often denotes generally 'coming
within the realm, sphere, or scope of the possessor', 'having
connexion with one', or even 'that one knows of or should know
of'. So in such examples as the following:

That was where I saw *my* first alligator.

Everybody should know *his* Shakespeare.

I am afraid he has not read *his* Bible.

We fired, and each of us killed *his* man.

She is not one of *your* blue-stockings.

Jog on, jog on, the footpath way,
And merrily hent the stile-a:
A merry heart goes all the day,
Your sad tires in a mile-a.—SHAKESPEARE

Special uses of the possessive adjectives follow those of the
personal pronouns to which they belong (see §185.1–4).

189   A possessive adjective or pronoun has sometimes a relative
depending on it; in such circumstances *my (mine), his, their
(theirs)*, &c. are mentally analysed as equivalent to *of me, of
him, of them*, &c.; e.g.

Nor better was *their* lot *who* fled.—SCOTT

Hard is *our* fate
Who serve in the state.—ADDISON

Let grief and sorrow still embrace *his* heart
That doth not wish you joy.—SHAKESPEARE

So far as it survives, this is a purely literary construction.

190   *Peculiarities*
1 In some connexions the equivalent with *of* is idiomatic,
in emotional use, where we should rather expect the possessive
genitive form to appear; e.g.

This loss will be the death *of me*.

For the life *of me*, I can't tell why.

That scoundrel of a nephew *of mine* . . .

This form is found to be especially appropriate in contemptuous
or threatening use:

I'll break the neck *of you*!

2 The usage with the noun *sake* shows a special peculiarity.
We do not normally say 'for the sake *of me*' or '*of them*', but
'for *my* sake', 'for *their* sake'; in groupings like the following,

however, we have usually the choice of two constructions: 'for the sake *of me* and the children', 'for *my* sake and the children's'.

3 'These are *three* friends *of mine*' and 'These are *three of my* friends' mean different things; the second implies that I have more than three friends; the first does not. So: 'In the study you will find *some* papers *of mine*', as opposed to: '*some of my* papers'.

191 Reflexive pronouns

1 The ordinary personal pronouns acquire reflexive meaning when they refer to the subject of the sentence or clause in which they occur:

> I pulled the ladder up after *me* (= *myself*).
> He made me move nearer to *him* (= *himself*).
> She had taken more and more responsibility upon *her* (= *herself*).

2 In earlier periods they were regularly used reflexively as the objects of *transitive* verbs:

> O Lord, haste *thee* to help me.

(This use is to be distinguished from that with *intransitive* verbs, as 'He sat *him* down' (§125).)

3 Today this function is performed by the forms compounded with –**self**, –**selves**; *myself, thyself, himself, herself, itself, oneself yourself, ourselves, yourselves, themselves*.

> How can I bring *myself* to do it?
> Pray do not inconvenience *yourself*.
> He believed *himself* to be possessed of miraculous powers.
> The Fathers contradict *themselves* and each other.

Twofold origin of forms compounded with –self

(i) In OE., *self* was properly a definitive adjective, which agreed with the pronoun to which it was joined; e.g. *ic selfa* (nominative) 'I self', *mīn selfes* (genitive) 'of me self', *mē selfum* (dative) 'to me self'. The dative combination, which was very common, early established itself as equivalent to the simple *self*; hence it was even joined to the nominative, perhaps as a kind of weakened dative of interest; e.g. *ic mē selfum = ic selfa*.

(ii) *Self* was also early used as a noun; so ME. *mī* (= *mīn*, genitive) *self* 'the self of me'. The forms derived from the genitive gradually supplanted the forms derived from the dative, both as a definitive adjective and as a reflexive pronoun. Thus we have *myself, thyself, yourself, ourselves, yourselves*. But in *himself, themselves* the forms derived from the dative have survived. (Compare however the dialectal *hisself, theirselves*.)

4 The forms in *–self* are also used in apposition with personal pronouns, by way of emphasizing them, as *I myself, you yourself, they themselves*.

5 By the omission of the personal pronoun these forms came to be used themselves as emphatic pronouns; this is archaic:

> *Myself* would work eye dim and finger lame.—TENNYSON
>
> Direct not him whose way *himself* will choose.
>
> —SHAKESPEARE

192   Interrogative pronouns and adjectives

1 *Who* and *whom* refer to persons only.

2 *What*, pronoun, being neuter, refers to things without sex.

3 *Which*, pronoun and adjective, and *what*, adjective, refer to both persons and things.

Examples:

> *Who* (*what*) is that? *Whom* (*what*) have we here?
>
> I do not know *which* of these two it is.
>
> Tell me *what* you are thinking of.
>
> Take it, no matter *whose* it is.
>
> *What* is the extent of the damage?
>
> *What* two people will be found to agree on this?
>
> *Which* man was it? *Which* is the house?

193   Relative pronouns: *who* (accusative-dative *whom*, genitive *whose*), *what, which, that, as*. **Relative adjectives:** *which, what*. In origin (i) *who, what*, and *which* are interrogative, (ii) *that* is demonstrative, and (iii) *as* adverbial. See §195.

194   1 In conversational language the commonest relative pronouns are *that, which*, and *who*; in the accusative *that* is preferred for persons, and *whom* is little used. Thus we tend to say 'the meeting *which* I attended yesterday', rather than 'the meeting *that* . . .'; and again, 'that sister of mine *that* you met' rather than 'that sister of mine *whom* you met'. But more frequently still we say 'the meeting I attended' and 'that sister of mine you met', the accusative relative being commonly omitted altogether (see §77).

2 The forms *whom* and *which*, in dependence on a preposition, are almost entirely confined to the literary style, since the use of *that* with the preposition detached and placed after the verb of the relative clause is particularly convenient for conversational purposes; and when the relative is not expressed, as frequently happens, we have a form of expression which can hardly be matched for conciseness in English or any other language. Thus we say 'the engineer (*that*) I was talking *about*', rather than '*about whom* I was talking'—'the word (*that*) you met *with*', rather than 'the word *with which* you met'.

3 But in the literary language *who* and *which* on the one hand, and *that* on the other, have acquired, within comparatively recent times, a distinction in usage which has been already dealt with in §76.

4 *Who* and *whom* refer to persons only. So also *whose* as a rule, but it is not infrequently found convenient to use *whose* in reference to things (= *of which*); in this way is avoided the somewhat awkward collocation of *of which* with the definite article: 'A large number of brass discs, *whose* workmanship (= the workmanship of which) shows that they belong to the later period of Celtic art, have been found in Ireland'.

5 *Which* often refers to the matter of a whole clause or sentence (= 'which fact or circumstance'):

The rain washed away the track, *which* prevented the trains from running.

6 *That* may be used as a relative adverb = 'on which', 'in which', 'at which':

I remember the day (*that*) he came.

On the day *that* thou eatest thereof thou shalt surely die.—*Bible*

7 *As* is used (i) as a correlative to 'such', 'same'; (ii) in expressions like 'beasts of prey, *as* lions and tigers'; (iii) = 'a thing or circumstance which'; e.g. 'He was a Russian, *as* they could tell by his accent'. (In vulgar speech *as* is the universal relative pronoun; it had formerly some literary standing.)

8 The relative adjective *which* is always equivalent to *and* (or *but*) *this* (or *that*), and these equivalents are now usually preferred as a matter of style. It is almost exclusively employed to qualify a noun repeated from the preceding sentence, and in the phrases *which last*, *which latter*.

The relative adjective *what* = *the*, *that*, or *those . . . which*; e.g. 'I showed him *what* clothes I should wear'. (Contrast 'I asked him *what* clothes I should wear': *what* is here interrogative and introduces a dependent question, §67.)

Note the poetical *what time* = 'at the time at which', 'when', an adverbial accusative used as a conjunction:

> . . . I made thee miserable
> *What time* I threw the people's suffrages
> On him that thus doth tyrannize o'er me.—SHAKESPEARE

195 1 *That* is the oldest of the relatives. In OE. it was neuter only, being the neuter of the demonstrative pronoun-adjective *sē, sēo, þæt,** which were combined with the indeclinable relative *þe*; thus *sē þe, sēo þe, þæt þe* = 'he who', 'she who', 'that which'. Ultimately *þæt* entirely supplanted *þe* as a universal relative.

2 The history of the use of *wh*-words as introducing relative clauses is peculiar. The words in OE. which functioned as relatives were in form demonstratives. Formerly one stood in each of the clauses; hence it is that there arose such combinations as *that that* = ModE. 'that which', 'what'. But in the 12th century we find that *wh*-pronouns (i.e. interrogatives) are beginning to take the place of the *th*-pronouns in the relative clause; this arose first in the oblique cases and in dependence on prepositions, no doubt because the existing demonstrative-relatives could not be used as oblique cases without ambiguity, *þe* being indeclinable, while *that* did not admit a preposition in front of it. The use of the *wh*-pronouns was subsequently extended to the nominative.

Table of Correlatives			
Interrogative	**Demonstrative**	**Relative**	
		individual	**general**
Pronouns who? what? which?	this that such the same	who what which that as as	whoever[1] whatever[1] whichever[1]
Adjectives what? which?	this that the such (a) the same	what which as as	whatever[1] whichever[1]
Adverbs how? when? where? whence? whither?	so now, then here, there hence, thence hither, thither the		as when where whence whither the

[1] Literary forms are also *whosoever* (*whomsoever, whosesoever*), *whatsoever, whichsoever.*

---

* *Sě, sěo, þæt* was (*a*) the OE. definite article; (*b*) a demonstrative and relative pronoun in the combinations mentioned in this paragraph.

3 The restriction of *which* to neuter antecedents is a comparatively modern one; cf. 'Our Father *which* art in heaven'.

4 *That* was formerly used = 'that that', 'that which', 'what'; e.g. '*That* thou doest, do quickly' (*Bible*).

5 *But* may be used = 'who (what or which) . . . not' when the main clause is negative or interrogative; e.g. 'There was not a heart (What heart was there?) *but* felt the pang of disappointment'.

196   Distributive and collective pronouns and adjectives

The following are used as pronouns and as adjectives: *any, one, other, another, each, either, neither, some, all, many, (a) few, enough, both, several, certain.*

Note the use of *one* as propword: Buy a good *one*; Is that the *one* you want? This *one* will do; the great *ones*; the Holy *One*; the Evil *One*.

The following are used as pronouns only: *anyone, everyone, someone, no one, none* (singular or plural); *anybody, everybody, somebody, nobody; anything, everything, something, nothing, nought.*

The following are used as adjectives only: *a, an* (indefinite article, see §201), *every, else* (e.g. *somebody else* = somebody other),* *no.*

197   When distributive or collective pronoun-adjectives precede a noun qualified by a possessive or demonstrative adjective, one construction only is possible now, except with *all* and *both*. We must say: '*each of his* (or *these*) pupils'; '*(n)either of his* parents'; '*none of his* friends'; '*many (most, any) of his* plans'. But we may choose between '*all his* time' and '*all of his* time', '*both his* hands' and '*both of his* hands'.

Formerly greater latitude prevailed in such connexions; e.g. Shakespeare has 'at *each his* needless heavings', 'of *every these* happened accidents'.

Contrast the word-order in '*all (of) his* time' and '*his whole* time'.

---

* Modern form of OE. *elles*, genitive singular neuter of Germanic stem *el-*, related to Latin *alius* 'other', used in such phrases as *āwiht elles* 'aught else', literally 'anything of other', and meaning either 'in addition' or 'as an alternative or a substitute'. With the first and second meanings it is used with *anything, nothing, anyone, no one, someone* (and the corresponding formations with *-body*); with the first meaning only it is used with *all* (pronoun), *much, little, a great deal*, and the like; in groups like *anyone else* it takes a genitive *'s*, e.g. *anyone else's*, which therefore contains what is historically a double genitive.

In *any, one, each, some, many, several, certain, none, of us* (*you, them, the company,* &c.), *of* has a partitive sense representing the old partitive genitive; this use of the preposition has been extended to *all of them*, in which it has no meaning, and which was expressed in OE. by *hī ealle* 'they all' (in later English replaced by *all they, they all*; cf. Latin *hi omnes* 'all these men'), beside which was the restrictive appositive *hī sume* 'they some', i.e. 'some of them'. We now say either 'they all' or 'all of them'; similarly 'you both' or 'both of you'.

Both our, both your, both their are sometimes used colloquially to mean *of both of us, of both of you, of both of them*; e.g. 'both our husbands' = 'the husbands of both of us'; similarly Shakespeare has 'both our mothers', 'both your pardons'. This reflects the ME. *our bōther, bōther our,* &c., in which both pronouns are true genitives. The need for a compact expression of this kind is often felt. We may sympathize with the little girl who, wishing to state that a certain pet was the common property of herself and her brother, said 'It's both of our donkey'!

The indefinite pronoun *who* (= 'someone') survives in the archaic 'as *who* should say' (= as though someone were to say).

198 The logical personal pronouns of reference to an indefinite pronoun (or noun) are *he, she, him, her, his, himself, herself. They, their, them, themselves* are, however, often used to avoid the awkwardness of *he or she, him or her, his or her, himself or herself.* So after *he or she.* Examples:

> Anyone may be a companion of St. George who sincerely does what *they* can to make *themselves* useful.—RUSKIN
> It's enough to drive anyone out of *their* senses.—SHAW
> A person can't help *their* birth.—THACKERAY
> One after another rose to express *their* opposition.
> Experience is the name everyone gives to *their* mistakes.
> —WILDE

For *you* and *we* as indefinite pronouns see §185.4.

The articles

199 The demonstrative adjective *the*, commonly called the definite article

1 *The* refers back to a person or a thing already mentioned or sufficiently identified; e.g.

> He built a great ship for himself and his companions . .
> *The* ship's name was Argo.

2 *The* identifies:

> I have *the* very thing you want.
> You mentioned a man in a white coat. This is *the* man.
> We shall claim either *the* one or *the* other.

3 *The* defines absolutely, that is, marks a person or a thing as (at the time) the only one so called, and is therefore regular in titles:

    the Lord (= God)   *the* Bible   *the* Scriptures
    the (river) Thames   *the* University of Oxford
    the first folio edition of Shakespeare
    the Archduke Charles   *the* Pope

So of the seasons of the year.

4 *The* marks a class or group, a collective whole:

    the mammalia   *the* military
    Youatt's book on *the* horse
    The private is in no way inferior to *the* officer in devotion
        to duty.

Observe, however, that we say 'man' not 'the man' in the sense of 'mankind'.

5 *The*, when strongly stressed, with a high tone, marks a person or a thing as unique:

    He is *the* pianist of the day.

In such use it is often printed in italics.

6 *The* is used with adjectives to form noun-equivalents (§17.3):

    the wise (= those who are wise)
    the good, *the* beautiful, and *the* true (= that which is
        good, beautiful, and true)

7 *The* is used with the plural of proper names (nations, classes, groups):

    the English   *the* Joneses

200 The definite article is suppressed when a noun to which it properly belongs is qualified by a genitive; thus 'a king's daughter' (= *the* daughter of a king), 'the boat's length' (= *the* length of the boat), 'a spear's length' (= *the* length of a spear), 'a stone's throw' (= *the* distance a stone can be thrown). 'A king's', 'the boat's', &c., are in fact 'group genitives' (§112); in OE. both article and noun would have the genitive inflexion.

Unlike many other languages, in which different genders may have to be expressed, English allows the omission of *the* with the later items in an enumeration, as in:

    the King and Queen   *the* Navy, Army, and Air Force

The insertion of *the* would have some special implication.

The is omitted before nouns like *school, church, college, hospital, chapel* when the activity referred to involves the use of the building for its particular purpose:

They are *at school*.
They are just coming *from chapel*.
He was taken *to hospital*.

201 The indefinite adjective *a, an*, **commonly called the indefinite article**

1 *A, an* is a reduced form of OE. *ān* 'one'. The meaning 'one' survives in expressions like '*a* foot high', 'wait *a* minute'; *a* is here less emphatic than *one* would be.

2 *A* singles out a person or thing and prepares us to hear something more about them:

Once upon a time there was *a* youth named Kilwych. Now Kilwych set out on *a* gray steed, strong of limb.

3 *A* has the indefinite meaning of 'any':

It is as big as *a* piece of chalk.
An island is *a* piece of land entirely surrounded by water.

4 *A* is distributive:

two shillings *a* pound (= each pound, per pound)
twopence *a*piece (for *a* piece, that is, any piece)

Adverbs

202 Adverbs should be so placed in a sentence as to make it impossible to doubt which word or words they are intended to affect. Observe in this connexion that qualifying words in English look *forwards* rather than backwards. Adverbs should therefore come if possible immediately before the words they qualify:

There is nothing that needs to be kept *more* within bounds.
Some were unwilling to grant *even* this favour.

A few adverbs, however, have a recognized place *after* the words to which they refer: e.g. *enough*, as 'good *enough*'; *only* in certain instances, as 'They *only* (= they and they alone) have come to this conclusion'; the adverbial phrase *at least*, as 'This *at least* is worth our notice'.

203 Normally, the adverb qualifying a finite verb follows it; e.g. He wrote *well*; cf. also §204. But some laxity is current in the placing of *only, merely, simply*:

I *merely* came to inform you of the fact. Instead of: I came *merely* to inform, &c.

He has *only* stayed for a week. Instead of: stayed *only* for
a week

'Came to inform', 'stayed for a week' are evidently treated as if they
were fixed groups.

204 When an adverb qualifies a compound tense its usual
position is between the auxiliary and the participle or the infinitive: 'We have *often* been here'; 'One should *always* get
up early'. But the adverb is not uncommonly held over to the
end of the sentence: 'We shall feel the blow *keenly*'; cf. 'We
felt the blow *keenly*'.

On sentence adverbs see §23.4.

205 The use of *not* in 'I hope *not*', 'I thought *not*', 'I should
say *not*', &c. is remarkable; it represents all that is left of a
subordinate clause, such as 'that it is *not* so'. It does not
strictly qualify 'hope', 'thought', &c. in the same way as in 'I do
not hope', 'I did not think', 'I should not say'. (But Latin in such
circumstances has 'Non spero', 'Non arbitrabar', &c.)

206 In modern English two negatives applied to the same word
or group neutralize one another. Thus we say: 'I have*n't* got
any', not 'I have*n't* got *none*'. But formerly double negatives
were common where a single one would be now used, and
sometimes quadruple negatives are found; e.g.

'Tis a discreet way concerning pictures in churches, to set
up no new, *nor* pull down *no* old.—SELDEN

He *nevere* yet *no* vileynye *ne* sayde
In al his lyf unto *no* maner wight.—CHAUCER

207 The is found as an adverb with comparatives, as in '*The*
more, *the* merrier' (see §101.4). It has (i) relative, (ii) demonstrative force: 'By *what* degree there are more, by *that* degree
they are merrier', Latin '*Quo* plures, *eo* hilariores'.

Conjunctions

208 Conjunctions are either co-ordinating or subordinating
(see §23.1–3).

And has a special idiomatic force in certain uses:

1 In expressions like 'This cloth is nice and soft', the first
adjective makes with the *and* an adverb-equivalent: almost
'nicely soft'. So with 'fine and . . .', 'lovely and . . .'.

2 Preceding a pronoun qualified by an attribute it sometimes forms an equivalent of a nominative absolute (see §98.4).

3 After *try* and before an infinitive *and* equals 'to':

Try *and* make your mind up.

We will try *and* find it.

209 The omission of **that** at the head of noun-clauses has been illustrated in §§60 foll. Formerly it was omitted much more freely and in circumstances where its omission would be now impossible or extremely awkward. Thus, in quoting *Genesis* ii 18, Hooker (about 1600) writes: 'It is not good man should be alone'. This appeared subsequently in the 1611 Bible as 'It is not good *that* the man should be alone'. Clarendon has: 'And it may be it was well they had not'—a form now characteristic rather of colloquial usage than of literary style.

Index

References are to *sections*.

b. Words

(*a* = adjective; *v* = verb)